Let The Earth Bring Forth

Other books by Mary Warren:

Westminster Press: (Juvenile)

Walk in My Moccasins
Shadow on the Valley
Eight Bells for Wendy
A Snake Named Sam
Ghost Town for Sale
River School Detectives
The Haunted Kitchen

Augsburg Press:

The Land of Christmas
On Our Way to Christmas
Lord, I'm Back Again

Concordia:

The City that Forgot About Christmas

Arch Book series:

The Great Surprise
The Lame Man Walks Again
The Great Escape
Boy With A Sling
The Little Boat that Almost Sank

Let The Earth Bring Forth

Mary Warren

Published by
chosen books
of The Zondervan Corporation
Grand Rapids, Michigan 49506

Scripture quotations used in this book are from the Revised Standard Version of the Holy Bible unless otherwise identified, and are used with permission.

LET THE EARTH BRING FORTH
Copyright ©1983 by Mary Warren

Library of Congress Cataloging in Publication Data
   Let the earth bring forth.

   1. Warren, Mary.   2. Converts—United States—Biography.   I. Title.
BV4935.W37A34 1983   289.6'092'4 [B]   83-7460
ISBN 0-310-60650-0

Printed in the United States of America.

Chosen Books is a division of The Zondervan Corporation, Grand Rapids, Michigan 49506. Editorial offices for Chosen Books are in Lincoln, Virginia 22078.

82 83 84 85 86 87 88 — 10 9 8 7 6 5 4 3 2 1

To Lindsay
and to Bishop Matthew Bigliardi
who so graciously welcomed us home

The world is charged with the grandeur of God.
  It will flame out, like shining from shook foil;
. . .
And for all this, nature is never spent;
  There lives the dearest freshness deep down things;
And though the last lights off the black west went
  Oh, morning, at the brown brink eastward, springs—
Because the Holy Ghost over the bent
  World broods with warm breast and with ah! bright
    wings.

(Excerpt from God's Grandeur
by Gerard Manley Hopkins
1876–1889)

Contents

	Preface	ix
I	The Desolate Places	11
II	Another Season	27
III	Silence	41
IV	Rock	51
V	Water	59
VI	Waiting	69
VII	The First Garden	79
VIII	Trees	91
IX	Small Things	101
X	The Other Side of Darkness	111
XI	Light	119
XII	Another Garden	127
	End Notes	137

A Gem Book
from Chosen

Preface

This is the story of a strange journey. I grew up in a Christian family and I never dreamed I would lose my faith. When it happened, I wandered in a spiritual wilderness for years.

Surprisingly, it was the elemental things of life— water, silence, spiders, earthworms, soil, roots, rocks, weeds and flowers—that finally turned me back to my Creator long before I was ready or willing to relate once more to human beings.

During my journey I learned that many others like myself have experienced doubt and despair and darkness and defeat regarding their lack of faith and inability to live victoriously. It is for such people this book is written.

Mary Warren

I

The Desolate Places

I

I am utterly spent and crushed;
I groan because of the tumult of my heart.

(Psalm 3:8)

Countless are the poems about the birth and death of families, countless the novels and songs. But the family of which I write was flesh and blood, a real mother and father and seven children.

Sourdough pancakes sizzled on the griddle in the morning. A real gingery-black mongrel barked at the children playing tag in the yard. Laughter echoed through the hall each night when the boys tramped upstairs to their attic "dormitory." And real teenage girls washed their hair in the shower, left clothing in heaps on the floor, and cuddled their baby sister before tucking her into the crib in the nursery.

The arguments and the fights were real, the good times and the bad.

How does a family break apart? How does it begin to crumble? I ask you truly, for this was my family, the husband and the children I loved.

I know one thing. The world around us had become a confusing place with strange new words falling heavy upon the tongue: marijuana and "speed," napalm, nuclear test site, assassination, dropout, runaway, vandalism, commune, detention.

Ours was a common problem but the facts in the nationwide surveys were of no comfort. As our youngsters entered puberty, the burden became too great. They ran from parental authority and they ran from themselves, trying anything, everything to ease their hurt.

Once I'd had a close relationship with my husband, Lindsay, a hospital chaplain. It deteriorated partly because we'd become so involved in the pain of our children that it was difficult to pay attention to each other's needs. Quite possibly our separation would have happened anyway. While one of us remained static, the other grew; and when both grew, it seemed to be in opposite directions.

I awoke before dawn one morning in a living nightmare. Our four oldest children had already left home. Now my husband was making the same decision.

Why should strangers continue to live together? And how had we become strangers?

I thought with anguish of the memories shared; laughter and tears; gifts given to one another. I ached for the small intimacies, the jokes, the long discussions into the early morning hours. In honesty, I recalled too the hurts withheld, the feelings disguised or never openly admitted.

I remembered special times with the children: the day we unexpectedly filled six new lunchboxes (before the last baby arrived) with blackberries as we picnicked near a pioneer schoolhouse in the country; the August ritual of buying bluejeans and pencils and writing tablets; the slumber parties and games of football; the filling of long, red Christmas stockings after the midnight Communion service.

That which had given meaning to my life, the constellation of family relationships, had shattered. The mother and father and seven children had been replaced by a mother and three children. The four of us were lonely and filled with a gnawing pain for the life we had shared.

Pain drew us together. But at the same time, it became a wall.

Then, too, I was discovering something worse than the alienation within my family. I who had been nurtured in the Christian gospel no longer believed in the existence of God. The seeds of disbelief had been sown long before Lindsay moved away into an apartment. Now, overwhelmed by despair and grief, I felt the full impact of my lack of faith.

Over the years, I'd grown discouraged with the wrangling I'd encountered among church members in the small Episcopal missions Lindsay had served as pastor. Too often, the concentration on picayune details frustrated me. ("How can we vote any money for flood victims when we need new dishes for our church kitchen?") My own beliefs had faltered. The gospel truths about love and salvation: how *did* they relate to devastating world events—nuclear bomb tests, the poisonous effects of insecticides, the war in Vietnam?

I thought back to the time I had been led into a vital faith, years ago during a summer session at the University of Colorado. Every Saturday evening the students in Canterbury Club, the Episcopal Church organization on campus, piled into cars and drove off into one of the nearby mountain canyons for a time of fellowship and fun. On weekdays, a smaller group of them attended the early morning Communion service in the tiny chapel behind the Canterbury House.

Those young people came from different backgrounds. Some were enrolled in the school of engineering; others expressed interest in art or medicine or teaching or journalism. I was surprised to learn how many of them, matriculating at a state university, readily admitted a call to the ministry.

Never before had I encountered college students, members of sororities and fraternities as well as Canterbury Club, who conversed about God as eagerly as they talked about dancing and mountain climbing. Often our late-night study sessions were interrupted by arguments over Bible passages and theology as we tested our ideas against those of the young, buoyant college chaplain, Father Pat.

By the end of the summer, Jesus Christ had changed from a remote figure living in another century to Someone who was affecting every portion of my life.

I ended up transferring my credits from the Ivy League college I'd been attending to Colorado University. After graduation I headed East once more to study on a graduate level at Union Theological Seminary in New York City.

When at last I met Lindsay, a senior at another seminary who was spending his Christmas holidays in the city, his eyes burned with the same fire I'd observed in the students at the Canterbury Club. Dark-haired and of medium height, he was enthusiastic about guitar-playing, medieval art, good jazz, calligraphy, Chinese food, bicycling, puns and poetry, his ongoing study of the Bible, and his deepening spiritual life. From the beginning, we shared on many levels, going for strolls and squandering nickels and dimes at a nearby automat, riding the subways, ending many a wonderful evening with prayer.

After he returned to his seminary in Ohio, letters flew back and forth almost daily. Then I flew back and forth, too, for a very special occasion: the Valentine dance weekend at which we announced our engagement.

Later, as newlyweds, we moved from the 200-year-old church in Elizabeth, New Jersey, where Lindsay first served as curate, to several small missions in Montana, and then on to Oregon.

Standing now in the middle of our Portland living room, I asked myself sadly what had destroyed that faith and that love. In addition to leaving home, my husband, a priest of fifteen years' standing, had decided to renounce his ordination vows.

I could not answer for him, but surely my own spiritual condition must be related to the lack of nourishment I was receiving from the Church; from the divisions I found in the world around me; from the

17

overpowering sense of the reality of evil; from the fact that my personal prayer life had disintegrated.

Luke tells us that, during the Passover, when the boy Jesus stayed in Jerusalem to talk to the teachers in the Temple, Mary and Joseph, "supposing him to be in the company . . . went a day's journey. . . ."

Quite without realizing it, I too had traveled a day's journey. I was no longer in the company of Christ. I could pinpoint no one moment, no particular day when I knew this to be true, but at last I admitted it. I was alone.

When words of prayer refused to come from my heart, I tried praying those age-old passages from the Psalms: "God is our refuge and strength, a very present help in trouble. . . ." "Lord, thou hast been our dwelling place in all generations. . . ."

But soon, joining the psalmist in his time of suffering, I cried out, "O Lord, my God, why hast thou forsaken me?"

After that I ceased to pray. How could I pray without any God to pray to?

Many have wandered in arid places. T. S. Eliot called it "the wasteland." Dante wrote of the dark wood, "so drear, so rank, so arduous a wilderness. . . . Its very memory gives a shape to fear."[1]

Death would have been easier to face than rejection by those I loved. I would have preferred it to the loneliness. Old friends did not come near me for a long time. Months passed before one of them called or wrote or dropped by. Later some of them confided: "We didn't know what to do." "We were afraid we might make matters worse by saying the wrong thing." "We felt too bad ourselves." "We thought you needed to be alone."

At first I was shocked at this apparent lack of concern,

but later it came to me: they had felt betrayed, and frightened. A staunch Christian family had broken into pieces. If it happened to the Warrens, well, it could happen to anyone. Even themselves.

When one or two of them tried to meet me halfway, it was my fault they failed. I was unable to handle the deep pain in their eyes, too centered in my grief, too certain that nothing would ever be right again.

The old way of life was gone forever. I looked into the void and felt terror, meaninglessness unconfined, endless, jarring, like the terrible noises people with a certain type of deafness hear constantly inside their heads. I tried to snare it in a poem called "Emptiness":

> When nothing-drums pound
> My tongue curls dry
> In a green-grape taste.
>
> Taut-wired,
> Stumble I down
> White corridors.
>
> Room opens into room
> Into room
> Into room
>
> But in this labyrinth
> What do I hear
> So raucously exploding?

On still another day, I attempted to give form to the grief I felt over my children:

"Graduation from Childhood"

The girl who made my birthday cake
  in the shape of a bonnet
  iced green with a garland of flowers
Has left home pregnant?

The boy—that impfaced one—
Hooked now?
       Please!

Tomorrow I may wake to find
Those innocent darlings giggling
In sleeping bags on my attic floor;
Or fishing for crawdads
From the foot bridge in the park.

Tomorrow I shall come upon them
Burning holes in report cards with
      a magnifying glass
Or caching club supplies—peanut butter,
      pickles, jam, crusts of bread
Under the porch steps.

That warp,
That plummeting to darkness
Happens to other people.

Listen! Do you not hear them
      shaking plums from the tree
      by the alley?
Is it the wind?

I remained without any real sense of the presence of
God for nearly two years. After that, although I could
not bring myself to say I believed in Him, I knew some-

thing had happened. But *what?* I had turned in a new direction.

The turning happened because of a pile of garbage!
In our small northwestern city, the residents pay a monthly fee to have rubbish collected. The rate is by the can. One can a week costs a certain sum; two cans cost more. Because my family had dwindled, and because we teetered on the edge of poverty, I could no longer afford to have two cans of garbage collected four times a month.

Our neighbor's garage had been turned into a "depot" for recyclable glass, newspaper, flattened cans and discarded aluminum foil. I began hauling boxloads of material over there. Then, after I had buried vegetable matter in one corner of our tiny backyard, there was little left to stuff into my trashcan.

It was an easy way to save money.

The unforeseen bonus gift did not grow out of my efforts to be frugal until the following spring. One day while digging a hole for a coffeecan full of potato peelings, orange skins, coffeegrounds and eggshells, I stooped to crumble a handful of earth between my fingers.

Where was the kitchen waste I had buried in previous months? It had vanished! In its place I discovered moist black soil. My next spadeful teemed with squiggly earthworms—minute worms as skinny as bits of red embroidery floss; larger ones; and those enormous nightcrawlers that make a fisherman's eyes light up in a hurry.

I had never been a gardener. Not a dedicated gardener, spellbound by the process of spading, planting, watering, weeding, reaping. The best I'd managed to do in the past was to bury a scattering of tulip and crocus bulbs along the shrubbery at the front of the house and then forget them until the flowers popped up in March. Now I refused to succumb to any vague impulse to take up gardening. But I did continue to bury garbage in one corner of my backyard.

Years would pass before I recognized this turning as a conversion. I thought, mistakenly, that conversions took place with startling speed, like the blinding of Saul on the Damascus road.

What happened to me was imperceptible. I knew only that the dreariness of each empty day had begun to be lightened by one small pleasure. The dark earth greeted me whenever I stepped outside to perform that simple task: spade the hole, bury the garbage and, in a few months, new soil!

I was participating in the creation process. Alone in the sunlight, the wonder of it seized me and I trembled. I became aware of an indescribable presence in the earth, the presence of life. The rhythm of birth and decay, birth and decay . . . and birth. . . .

I remained suspicious of people. If those who had meant the most to me could wrench and hurt, it might happen again with others. I was unwilling to risk. But the day I discovered the carrot peelings gone and held a clump of new soil in my hand, I began to have faith in *something*. I called it faith in the presence-of-life-within-the-earth.

The planet had survived the scarring of centuries, the storms and battles, volcanoes and glaciers and floods. If earth contained the power within itself to endure, then might I not find the same power within myself?

It was a first step, this realization that I might endure disintegration and move beyond it. But how?

Often I was consumed with self-hatred. I knew I was partly responsible for the rejection I experienced. But no matter where the blame rests, rejection always hurts. It is a humiliating blow to our self-esteem when we realize that the people we love do not want to be around us anymore.

I did not want to live in a half-family. It made me heartsick to think of doing so, perhaps for the rest of my life. I lost myself in depression. Life seemed cruel; not only my life, all life.

How could anyone believe in a loving God when great leaders like Martin Luther King, Jr., had been gunned down? When innocent Vietnamese children had been maimed with napalm? When people in Bangladesh and Calcutta starved while Americans fretted over the soaring prices of coffee and beef?

I raged over the unspoken anguish of runaway youngsters, our children, anyone else's children; and over the thousands of elderly people restrained in nursing home beds.

Why, why, why the greed, the bitterness, the rejection? I was too distraught to read deep books, too confused to take part in any meaningful dialogue. Grief had thrown my thoughts into a tangle.

What I longed for most was a rest from the human relationships that had gone awry. I yearned for oblivion. But suppose death did come, bringing with it another life?

It seemed impossible to find a responsible way out of my dilemma. I was surrounded by people whether I wished to be or not: a son and a daughter, both in junior high; a lively preschooler; neighbors in such close proximity that we could use sign language to communicate through our side windows.

This one short city block housed twenty-nine young-sters!

And so I was caught in the middle of a daily pressure to relate to others. I felt *terrible*. My posture showed it, and the tears in my eyes, and the catch in my voice. Whenever I did attempt to mask my feelings, they clamored for recognition.

A wise therapist helped me try to cope with depression. Rather than masking the depression with tranquilizers, he wanted me to be able to "feel it through."

"In fact," he said, "when your depression is at its worst, sit down in a chair and *wallow* in it."

Rollo May puts it another way. He says, in *Love and Will*, that when we turn and face our most terrifying feelings head-on, and befriend them, they lose their grip upon us.

A strange idea, to become friends with your own depression! And yet, in my case, it worked. It involved a week spent in the crisis unit at the University Hospital, and countless hours in the doctor's office; but in the end those debilitating periods of depression disappeared forever.

It definitely did help to sit down in a chair and give myself permission to feel depressed. On one never-to-be-forgotten day, something special happened. It dawned on me that my family wasn't everything. An entire universe existed, waiting to be explored!

Startled, I got up and went outside in the sunlit yard, and began to watch the ants.

Now here is a person whose husband had moved away, whose children were destroying themselves sniffing glue and, far worse than that, gasoline; breaking into houses; constantly on the run. And what did she do? She sat out in the backyard observing ants.

Was she crazy?

That is the question I asked myself that day. And I realized the answer was no. I wasn't crazy. I was more sensible than I had been for ages. In the quiet of the yard, I was coming to grips with a difficult, most astounding thought: *I had idolized my husband and my children.*

For fifteen years I'd been so wound up in the intricacies of family life that I'd forgotten how to relate, in any significant way, to the rest of the world. I'd forgotten how to consider myself as an individual person. I saw myself always as mother or wife.

Several times since then, friends facing broken marriages have said to me, "But my husband and my children have been my entire life. How *could* this happen to me?"

And with all the gentleness I can muster, I answer, "Don't you see? That is probably one of the reasons it *did* happen."

My family, a large portion of it, anyway, had rejected me. But the universe had not. The world was at my fingertips. Why not become acquainted with it?

I sat in the grass playing with the idea of rejection and acceptance. Ants, of course, are incapable of feeling emotion. But, in a very real sense, they could accept or reject my giant foot. When I remained perfectly still they crawled over my shoe and hurried on. Some of them tickled their way across my outstretched hand.

The bee collecting pollen from the weeds at the edge of the yard did not sting me when I showed no fear. It, too, accepted me. Nearby a robin spied a worm in a dirt clod and ignored me as it hopped over to tug it out.

I remained in the backyard for hours, lost in thought, my pain dispelled, my loneliness set aside. I was not anyone's wife or mother right now. I was not the author of several books in the public library. I was me, without any title at all.

In one place at least, in this matchbox-sized yard, I was accepted. The ants continued to meander across my tennis shoe; and the robin, having devoured his worm, settled for a shower in the neighbor's sprinkler.

II
Another
Season

II

For everything there is a season and a time for every matter under heaven.

(*Ecclesiastes 3:1*)

Most of us seldom notice the unseen mysteries beneath our feet. Thousands of earthworms move tons of soil each year, literally *tons* of it, making it possible for the blue hydrangea bush, the roses, the grass, the clover, the starlike English daisies to flourish. To a large extent, food crops and flowers, orchard, meadow and forest depend on these lowly creatures.

29

One morning, after digging into the damp ground, I held an earthworm. I knew nothing about him but I was eager to learn. Soil-builder, herald of the presence of life-within-the-earth, it fascinated me.

Armed with a formidable stack of library books, I sat out on the back steps to do research.

An earthworm has no sense of smell. No ears; no eyes. Surprisingly, it possesses not one but several hearts and a rudimentary brain. Its sense of touch is phenomenal. The special collar of nerves encircling a worm's neck enables it to discern the difference between daylight and darkness, and to recognize various vibrations: the light, quick hop of a thrush, or human footsteps.

An earthworm breathes through its skin. At times it uses its pointed head for a digging tool. Usually it eats its way through the soil instead. Rotting leaf bits and other organic matter pass through the worm's digestive tract after being stored for a while in the crop. When food reaches the gizzard, it is ground up before it travels on down a long tube. Special juices help the worm digest food.

I glanced up from my books. Blackberry vines roamed in a tangle throughout the unpruned laurel hedge. Rosebushes, straggly and uncared for, bloomed near a rusty swingset. At the other end of the yard, a swivel chain had been screwed into the grass so our mutt, Timmy, could bask in the sun and watch the children play. The unkempt yard mirrored my distaste for life.

And then the earthworm began to reveal important secrets. It told me much was going on in the world, totally unrelated to my bruised feelings. I was a speck in the universe. If I died tonight and all my problems with me, the world would move right along as if no significant event had occurred.

A disconcerting thought? No. But humbling, because it forced me to deal with my false sense of self-importance. The worm symbolized the reliability of the creation process. Millenia before any of us were around to toss pancakes or drive children to swimming lessons, earthworms were moving soil. Generations pass, nations vanish, and their tunneling continues.

The earthworm presented me with a fresh awareness of the strange mixture of simplicity and complexity running through creation. A crumb of dirt, viewed by man's naked eye, is only a crumb of dirt. Seen through another lens, it is alive with bacteria.

I was too poor to buy a bag of apples but the ground in my backyard burgeoned with riches. Throughout the year, in proper season, hundreds of eggs burst open. Flies unfolded iridescent wings. The fragrance of roses filled the air. Roots stirred, seeds cracked and sprouted, ants sped through the streets of cities unknown to any human being. Spiders wove gossamer webs.

Though I ached with a personal sorrow and with that of a wounded planet, beauty had never been absent. It existed side-by-side with the most malevolent ugliness. Side-by-side? More than that. Sometimes the ugliness appeared to be *shot through* with beauty. It depended on what one brought to it from oneself, and how one assimilated the experience.

I was prompted to look again at the garbage in my life. Always I'd been a hot-tempered person, skillful in the art of sarcastic retort. Wanting things my way. Creative, yes. And a person with a passable sense of humor. But, at this moment, the garbage had choked out other more amenable traits.

Pain, if allowed to do so, demolishes. Yet we meet or read of those who have come through potentially ravishing experiences more whole. After the Holocaust, a Polish friend of mine went on to graduate from an American university *summa cum laude* and enter medical school. Corrie ten Boom was able, in the end, to love those who had destroyed her family during concentration camp years. And Helen Keller claimed victory over a world both soundless and dark.

There is buried within us a force strong enough to combat that which is negative and evil. If we let down the barriers and say yes, this force will do the "earthworm work" and fertilize our interior soil.

When had I last looked at a dandelion or felt the wind crinkling my nostrils? I thought with sadness of the years rushing by, the sheer waste: those years I had seldom noticed dewdrops or dogwood, or the new moon riding overhead among the stars, or the sunrise bannering the morning sky.

I could write books and bake a German chocolate cake, but how ignorant I was when it came to recognizing members of the sparrow family, one from another! As for the stars—on a clear night, ask me to point out the two dippers, the North Star, Jupiter and sometimes Mars. No others.

Most of us are destitute in this respect, having lost any real sense of relationship to the universe. We of the twentieth century attack our surroundings with snowmobiles and other expensive machinery. Few of us, however, have learned to sit quietly and be cognizant of a single rose.

Life continues, said the earthworm. Life moves on.

That is not what I wanted to happen! I clutched the past, a past that was out of reach now. I had not learned to let go of memories and loved ones, traditions, the little things that had melded nine of us into a family a short time ago. Clay horses and birds lined one windowsill, reminders of school art projects. Reminders of the children who had gone away.

I could not tolerate the sight of these things, but neither could I bring myself to store them in the blanket chest in my bedroom. Lindsay's colorful preaching stoles, purple and white, green and red, were at the bottom of that chest. As a young pastor, he had designed the emblem on the green one, a red triangle with a basket of loaves and a fish superimposed upon it. Painstakingly, I had embroidered the design, outlining each part with gold thread.

The Bible my father had given to me was in the chest, too, beneath a stack of blankets. "It is filled with stories of another day," I told myself. "Men and women who lived thousands of years ago. What difference can they make to me? My life is *now*."

The Bible stayed buried beneath the blankets. But after I began to live outside the Hebraic-Christian tradition, I found no way to prevent familiar stories and verses from flitting through my mind like persistent ghosts.

The story of Lot's wife appeared, unbidden.

Lot's wife, after being ordered not to look back, did so and turned into a pillar of salt. The truth contained in that brief statement had never become clear to me until recently. Chained to the past, I too was in danger of freezing, exactly like a pillar of salt!

Life continues, said the earthworm. Life moves on.

"Live each season as it passes," wrote Thoreau in his journal on August 23, 1853. "Breathe the air, drink the drink, taste the fruit, and resign yourself to the influence of each."

"Live each day as it passes." Does this mean we must permit ourselves to be trampled and smashed in the process? I think not. Surely Thoreau meant don't *waste* a season merely because it is a harbinger of pain.

Carl Jung, the Swiss psychiatrist, wrote: "We must be able to let things happen in the psyche. For us, this actually is an art of which few people know anything. Consciousness is forever interfering, helping, correcting, and negating, and never leaving the simple growth of the psychic processes in peace. It would be simple enough, if only simplicity were not the most difficult of all things."[2]

Certain life experiences, usually the ones overwhelming us with a deep sense of sorrow or joy or awe, and sometimes terror . . . have a way of pruning us down to our most basic selves. Peeled to the essential unmasked *me*, I experienced a new kinship with the earth. By getting in touch with the earth, I was as getting in touch with my humanity as never before. Suddenly I understood why the words *humus* and *humble* and *human* shared a common root.

During times of crisis, life around us changes so quickly that it can be very confusing. Readily, we identify with Alice in Wonderland in her reply to the Caterpillar's question, "Who *are* you?"

"I hardly know sir," she answered, "just at present—at least I know who I *was* when I got up this morning, but I think I must have changed several times since then."[3]

Later on, in *Through the Looking Glass*, she told the White Queen, "One *can't* believe impossible things."

"I daresay you haven't had much practise," said the

Queen. "When I was your age, I always did it for half-an-hour a day. Why, sometimes I've believed as many as six impossible things before breakfast."[4]

I had lived through another summer and fall. Down by the school, children leaped and scuffled through red-gold piles of leaves. At the other end of our block, a seagull flew in from the river to perch on the steeple of the red brick Lutheran church—a sign stormy days were approaching.

Yes, I had survived several seasons, and silently I admitted I must have taken a few steps without knowing it. I did believe four impossible things, and that was something. Four out of six:

My husband, once warm and full of zest, had become a stranger.

Disillusioned, he had renounced his ordination vows.

I, too, wandered in a meaningless world.

And our family had fragmented.

As I mentally listed these impossible things, I wondered what the other two would be. Did I have the stamina to endure more? I thought so. I was beginning to toughen up. I'd been given a peek at what looked like a fifth impossible thing and it warmed my heart to discover that this one, unlike the others, brought with it a degree of hope: in the midst of the rotting compost of my life, new seeds were starting to grow!

The question remained, though: how would I fill the long and empty days? I was not the Brownie leader type, or a member of clubs and bowlings teams.

The answer came through an unexpected gift. My son arrived home from school with a birdfeeder.

"Look what I made in shop!" he exclaimed proudly. "I want to put it up right now. Where would you like it—outside the kitchen window?"

"All right," I agreed, without the heart to mention there would be no grocery money left over for birdseed.

Before long, a sturdy pole had been hammered into the hole dug for it and the feeder was attached carefully to the top.

"And now," my son announced cheerfully, "I'll go get that dollar I've been saving for seed."

When you look through a window, you are not looking at yourself anymore. You are looking outward. And looking outward, might this not be considered the same as taking a step?

In the morning, after rinsing off the breakfast dishes, I stared at the feeder. In a few days the Peterson *Western Bird Guide* lay open on the counter while I puzzled over three different kinds of sparrow.

I knew the slim bird with the reddish purple head was a house finch. A longtime lover of fairy tales, I preferred the lilting name used in the old stories, *linnet*. The plain plump brown bird with striped belly turned out to be the linnet's mate. Seldom did the male dine at the feeder without her.

I began to rise early, before the children wakened, to watch what went on at the feeder. I moved, as always, from the refuge of sleep to the waking realization that the events of the past months were true. When my eyes were open, I would face a cockeyed world riddled with grief. And yet, as if to deny it, the chickadees and sparrows who had learned to recognize my shadow danced to the feeder as soon as I entered the kitchen.

Soon I was performing extra tasks to please them,

setting flowerpot saucers of water where they could be spotted; soaking stale crusts in meat drippings; preparing a popper of corn just for the gluttonous jays.

Next spring I would leave tag ends of string on the shrubbery for nest builders. I would oblige the robins by providing a supply of mud for their architectural projects. I did not plan to go as far as one of our daughters. In Montana, as a chubby little girl, she had tried making nests from mud and sticks and grass. These she left around "for any lost birds who needed them."

When I could afford it, what type of shrub would be appreciated near the feeder? Did every finch or flicker possess an individual personality so that a watchful person might tell them apart from other members of their species? I had read that geese mate for life. How many other birds did that? My mind overflowed with questions.

Too long, our scientific age has relegated healing to the domain of professional people. Life itself offers many avenues of restoration. Birds have no license to heal, nor does a compost heap full of worms. Neither, for that matter, does an eighth grade youngster hammering together a birdfeeder. But the birds, and the boy coming with his gift, were ointment for my wounded spirit.

If I could spend a few moments intent on what was transpiring outside the kitchen window each day, and add to these another moment . . . and another . . . perhaps I would find myself out of the darkness for longer periods of time.

In the crisp, late autumn air, I began to enjoy a second cup of coffee on the back steps, saying out loud: "Everything else may be depressing, but this cup of coffee is delicious."

By savoring each drop, I was able to make the coffee last for fifteen minutes. After that I walked the baby, a toddler now, ten blocks to the park, paying close attention to the leaves and pebbles she collected along the way. Nothing is quite as refreshing as a leisurely walk with a small child. Hardly a crack in the pavement goes unexplored.

Daily we played on the swings, drank from the fountain, somersaulted over the soft grass. In the process, I realized how much of one's depression is linked with ingratitude.

Home again, I folded a piece of paper in half. On one side I wrote the miserable things that had happened, on the other side the gifts life had given to me. The second list ended up running right off the page. I'd included everything imaginable: daisies and bumblebees, homemade bread, the laughter of small children, clean sheets and hot baths, reading in bed at night, bonfires on the beach, snowflakes and minnows, shafts of sunlight, and the sound of rain.

That insight helped. But the afternoons continued to stretch frighteningly empty. I made a plan to treat them the same way as the mornings, concentrating on blocks of time: put the baby down for her nap, bake a batch of gingersnaps or a pan of apple crisp; do two loads of laundry. Mundane time-fillers.

"What do I smell?" the seventh-grader sang out as soon as she entered the house the day I put this plan into action.

"It's been ever so long since we've had any of these," commented her brother, busily stuffing cookies into his pockets.

The scheme was a rousing success until I recalled that

another empty day would face me tomorrow. And a series of days and months and years after that.

I tried to remember Thoreau and his seasons, and to convince myself that the rough part would be over after a while. But before I could draw a breath, I saw the fallacy. *The rough days might be the only ones available. These were the days I must drink fully of. No others.*

Buried garbage. For the earthworm, it had the potential of new soil.

III

Silence

And behold, the Lord passed by. . . .

(*I Kings 19:11*)

The birds opened the way to silence. Birds are skittery creatures, alarmed by the slightest commotion. In order to watch them, I must learn to be very quiet.

In one of his *Quartets,* T. S. Eliot remarks that "ease is the cause of wonder."[5] The silence toward which I moved—how wonderfully easy it was to receive at last! But without the stripping first, there would have been no way to hold it.

43

It was not the enchanting inner silence so dear to children, but more akin to that found in open spaces: the quietness of the Arizona desert, or the silence of a meadow under the stars.

Invading a cluttered life, it caught me off-guard.

When farmers let a field lie fallow, something happens in the empty field. The green stuff, permitted to grow there freely, rots. And through the mysterious work of worm and bee and beetle, infinitesimal bacteria, rain and sun—new life infiltrates the worn-out soil.

Jung was right. We need to rest sometimes, like the fallow fields; to do nothing for a while, and to absorb the silence.

Some of us need silence more than others. When I was growing up, I felt different from my playmates because I craved an inordinate amount of time alone. After a few happy-go-lucky games of hide-and-seek and hopscotch, I sneaked away to "do my thinking." This was what I called those long hours of inactivity. The grownups used a derogatory expression: daydreaming.

More than dreaming, it was my method of becoming acquainted with the deep-down self I scarcely knew, a self that surprised and shocked, a self capable of weaving fantastic stories whenever I could bring myself to be utterly still.

The stories and poems appeared readily during summers spent at my grandfather's home on Long Island. Here, on warm afternoons, I rowed out into the swiftly running current of West Meadow Creek, dropped anchor, and sat slapping flies, waiting in a world caught in a golden net of light. More stories came after dark, during the long pause between the end of the cricket concert and the mournful whistle of the midnight train.

I learned how to visit with my inner self anytime I wished, simply by tuning out commotion. In math class or church, or during a subway rush, it was always possible.

Too often, I protected myself by retreating inward. On the other hand, I developed a kind of stamina, a self-knowledge many people long for and fail to find because they've never known true solitude.

From the moment today's children enter nursery school and plummet into first grade and after-school latchkey programs, Scouts, summer camps and clarinet lessons, they seldom have an opportunity to be alone.

"Jodie hates weekends," the mother of a four-year-old confided. "She doesn't know what to do with herself without nursery school. She is used to having something going on every minute."

I feel sorry for the Jodies of the world. My sister and I shared a room up to the time our older brother joined the Navy. But still our parents met our need for privacy by giving each one of us a special desk. Mine had belonged to my grandmother. Both the slanting lid and the cupboard door hiding four deep drawers at the side could be locked. So, in the city where no rowboat could provide an escape, I had my desk in the corner of the bedroom, a place to sit undisturbed and "do my thinking."

Years later, when one of our three sons required large blocks of solitude, I was not rattled. His teacher, however, showed little sympathy.

"Mrs. Warren, he doesn't play well with other children. That is why I had graded him low in social skills. He is such a dreamer! Why, the other day when he was out at the far end of the schoolyard, he didn't pay the slightest attention to the bell!"

"That must have been the afternoon he saw a mother spider carrying her babbies piggyback," I protested, wondering privately how many students, or teachers for that matter, had seen the same thing. "He told me about it, later. He's always running in to tell us about rainbows and clouds."

"But the bell had rung," his teacher reminded me reproachfully.

Schedule bells are necessary, of course, but not always. We need to know when and why they are useful. And when some deep vision calls . . . do we pay attention to the schedule bell or the rainbow? It is a question worth asking.

Childhood is filled with these visionary silences. As we mature, we experience others, too: the expectant silence of a theatre audience waiting for the curtain to rise; the silence born of fatigue after a heavy day's work; the creative silence familiar to artists, poets, scientists and others on the verge of a breakthrough.

Still another silence is that shared with a loved one when we've reached the level where speech is no longer necessary.

Dialogue is crucial to a healthy relationship, but space and the honoring of a person's need for space is equally important.

One summer before I was married, I worked at a Navajo mission in Arizona. Often an interpreter drove me into the desert to call on isolated families. We said nothing as we entered each hogan. The Navajo custom was to keep silent for perhaps half-an-hour or more before a few words of greeting were exchanged. When I became used to it, this had a marvelously quieting effect. Before I returned to the city, I had discovered the depth to be found in nonverbal friendship.

Years later my husband, a master calligrapher, observed that the space between letters is as vital to the beauty of a calligraphed passage as the exquisitely formed letters themselves.

Like any other couple, we had shared silence traveling in the car, sitting before an open fire, sipping our afternoon tea. But the silence of the past few years was different. It was empty, despairing, spawned of loneliness and opposition. Brittle, with a hostility seldom erupting into words.

In our alienation we had nothing left to say. The silence between us was no longer an open space in which two spirits moved. It had become a wall.

Solitude and loneliness are not synonymous. Solitude is connected to how we relate to our inner space, and to ourselves. Loneliness has to do with one's *lack* of relationship to other human beings. Often it has to do with one's stunted relationship with oneself and, although I was unable to define it at the time of which I write, the loss of any meaningful relationship to that-which-is-greater-than-self. God.

I was not experiencing true solitude anymore, but loneliness. Solitude nourishes, but loneliness, unless we have the inner strength and clear vision of a Teilhard Chardin or an Einstein, is very apt to tear down and destroy.

Why does God seem to be absent from us at the very time we need Him most? Jesus said, "Ask, and it will be given you; seek, and you will find; knock, and it will be opened to you."[6] But there are those times when we knock and every door remains closed; when we ask and more questions come instead of answers. And, in our constant seeking, what do we find? Nothing more than a way of separation, pain, terror, emptiness.

That, at least, is how I felt for a long time. I know I am not alone, for I have talked to others who have wandered in this godless way.

The silence within me, related now to loneliness, no longer fed me. It threatened. I wanted to get away from it but did not know where to turn.

And then the birds began to lure me!

Each time I felt oppressed, I went outside and traded the heavy silence for the light and shining silence of the natural world. I could bear the quietness of a blue sky, a cloud. I could bear the silence of tree shadows dancing across the sidewalk. Whenever I was in the yard, contentment scattered my unfulfilled longings to the wind. Open, I waited to be filled by that greatest of all silences, the vast cosmic silence stealing upon us so quietly we do not recognize it at first.

The world, that painful, clutching world, fell away and I stood free. A child of the universe.

I could look upon the scene outside myself with a quiet mind. More than that, I found myself *participating* in the silence. Parched, I let it lave over me. Empty, I allowed myself to be filled. This was a silence to be received, and it was beautiful beyond telling.

The winter was almost over. One day when I stepped into the yard, every twig and blade of grass was motionless, waiting for spring. Winters in western Oregon are raw and wet and cold, but as I stood looking this day, the sunlight glistened on the rooftops and the leafless trees. It made each puddle shine.

Quiet the world about me. And quiet my heart. Quiet!

And then it happened. The silence within me, the

deep, creative silence I'd thought to be gone forever, rose up to greet the silence being given and to welcome it with joy.

It was a gift. I knew this as certainly as I stood there on firm ground. But how could there be a gift . . . without a Giver?

IV
Rock

IV

He drew me up from the desolate pit, out of the
miry bog, and set my feet upon a rock,
making my steps secure.

(Psalm 40:2)

The tranquil moments spent observing birds and
drinking in silence were transitory. Much of the time I
had the sense that I was slipping . . . slipping.

When a major earthquake occurs, the land is altered
beyond recognition. Such a disruption is frightening.
Yet the survivors endure, rebuild, go on.

A radical shift in lifestyle is like that. The total land-scape is uprooted. There is nothing firm or dependable to hang onto anymore.

One small part of me withstood the shattering, a hard inner core, an essential me that refused to be pul-verized, like the rock I picked up to hold one day.

Familiar things had changed character—the house, for instance. The furniture in the room off the dining room had been rearranged. It became my writing study instead of my husband's den. He'd taken a few belong-ings over to his apartment and had given much away. The house did not seem like a couple's home anymore: no men's shoes to trip over on the bedroom floor; no forgotten coffee mug on the mantel; no calligraphy pens, sermons and books strewn around; no clerical collars perched in strange places.

What was *real* to me now?

The little stone in my hand was real. It would not melt away like my former life. A rock set down on a desk today will be there tomorrow.

The rocks in my yard had been there for centuries. Perhaps in another age an Indian had held one of those very rocks, examining it to see if it might make a strong tool.

Rock has always been an integral part of man's exis-tence. His first dwelling was a cave, his first altar a pile of stones. Rocks have provided spears, sharp cutting knives, arrowheads, axes, hammers and chisels, stat-ues, pieces of jewelry, gravemarkers, pyramids, castles, cathedrals, cisterns, roads. Primitive people in many cultures prized their grinding bowls and flat grinding stones or metates so highly that it became customary to hand them down from generation to generation.

Pebbles have been used in games as marbles and

counters. People have scratched messages into rock, and have painted pictures upon it. Not only Jacob, but many another traveler has chosen a smooth flat rock for a pillow when forced to camp in a lonely place far from home.

A stone often symbolizes the inner self, and also the divine. Is it so strange, after all, that we find comfort and pleasure in holding smooth small stones? Nor is it strange that in a sophisticated age when man-made materials have usurped its place, we still seek devious ways to renew our relationship with rock—by carving the faces of famous men on cliffs, and by becoming rockhounds and mountain climbers.

References to stone abound in myth and poetry, alchemy, history, literature. The amulets of ancient societies, the magic pebbles found in fairy tales the world over, the stories of statues shedding real tears are but a few examples. The Bible contains frequent allusions to it. I did not need to go upstairs and dig out my copy of Holy Scripture to know that. I had memorized many verses in Sunday school as a child. Sometimes in the yard, they came to mind.

"The Lord is my rock, and my fortress, and my deliverer," sang David, "my God, my rock, in whom I take refuge."[7]

Still another passage I could not forget was one I'd heard used as a sermon text at some time: "You were unmindful of the Rock that begot you, and you forgot the God who gave you birth."[8]

The pebble in my hand gleamed white and was cool and smooth to the touch. I heard a voice (was it *my* voice?) saying, "Be thou my rock. Be thou my rock."

A four-word prayer. It was the sixth impossible thing;

so great had been my disbelief, my journey through the wilderness until now!

The prayer sprang up of its own accord, a green shoot in a barren land. When I looked at my life I found other shoots. Fragile they were. Oh, how easy it would have been to trample them down or to miss them entirely. But with persistence they poked through the rich and crumbly dark new soil of my innermost being.

Because of a compost heap, I could say I believed in the presence of life-within-the-earth, and in the power of that life to renew itself. The earthworm supported this belief, assuring me that the planets would continue to orbit the sun, and cherry trees would blossom regardless of my personal emotional turmoil. The sense of anonymity gained from the insight might have proved destructive had it not been balanced by a glimpse into another paradoxical truth: man and his universe are interconnected.

I was a link in an ongoing creative process. One grain of sand is unnoticeable; but remove one hundred grains from a spot and you have an indentation, however small. Each grain does matter.

"For a soul to have a body is to be *enkekosmismene*," said Teilhard Chardin.[9] *Rooted in cosmos.*

I was rooted in cosmos. I mattered!

A few sparrows and finches had flung open the door to silence, and the silence on that never-to-be-forgotten afternoon had left me with the certainty of something worth exploring, beyond the disrupted portion of the world careening crazily around me; something larger than the toothpick figures and haunted eyes of the famished on the TV newscasts; larger than prisoners of war and murder and pollution, and all the other man-made terrors; larger than my personal suffering.

For a long time I had hesitated to call that something *God*. But the four words *Be thou my rock* said more than "God exists." *Be thou* acknowledged He was Person. And *Be thou my rock*, the entire phrase, signified that He was capable of caring.

When you are in some way related to the universe, your life takes on a degree of significance; and when a person cares about you, you are not anonymous anymore.

I was beginning to believe again! I wanted to shout so the news would be carried on the wind. Instead I laughed, startling a small daughter into a fit of giggles.

I had to admit that the complexities I saw around me could be nothing less than a work of love. Could a thumb or an eyeball or an earthworm with several hearts evolve by happenstance?

Such a breakthrough into the realm of belief brings with it not only a freshness and a glow but a new dilemma. One wishes to share it, to communicate, to give it form in a letter or poem or work of art.

I was not ready to seek out like-minded people. Had someone invited me to go to church at this point, I would have drawn back. Lest anyone else be trapped into thinking his steps toward belief are too slow and faltering, let me point out that God, in my case, neither pushed nor pulled.

The Bible bids us to wait upon the Lord. For me it seemed to be the other way around. The Lord of the universe waited for *me*. He was in no hurry. Why should He be? He had eternity.

V
Water

V

*Blessed is the man . . . who going through the vale
of misery use it for a well; and the pools
are filled with water.*
> *(Psalm 84:5-6, Book of Common Prayer)*

To supplement a meager income, I started a writing
workshop. Eight adults met weekly around my dining
table.

"You need to prune your rosebushes," commented a
student, peering out my study window. "And as soon

as the danger of frost is over, you should loosen the dirt and fertilize. Manure, you know, or compost."

So there I was in March, kneeling with bucket and trowel and shears—no gardener, I—wondering how to do the pruning. Did one start anyplace?

"Trim more than that," advised my neighbor. "Much more. Here, let me show you. The more you prune, the healthier your roses will be next June."

"A clove of garlic planted between each rosebush deters aphids," instructed the green-thumb student the following week. "That isn't an old wife's tale, either. It works."

"If anyone wants a root of mint, I've got plenty to give away," volunteered another student during the lull between manuscripts when we were pouring a second round of coffee.

"Mint tea sounds delicious," I heard myself say. "I'd like a few roots, please."

In our part of the country, because of rich soil and wet weather, shrubs, trees, flowers and fern bloom profusely with a minimum of fuss. Or so I thought, never having been interested before.

"But care does make a difference," promised the students as they started home, their notebooks and portfolios under their arms. "Compost helps, and the pruning."

"I see you have tulips coming on after the daffodils," commented one, pausing on the sidewalk in front of the house.

Green shoots inside and out! And writing workshop students who had grown up on farms, some who had won prizes in local garden club exhibits. I'd started out to teach a group of adults how to break into print and here I was, a raiser of mint and garlic and roses!

Until I pruned the roses, the yard had taken care of itself, except for a biweekly mowing of grass and a little careless spading here and there. Now that I'd invested effort in those shrubs and in the mint and garlic, I hoped for a modicum of success. Out came the hose, and up went my water bill.

Never once had water been a scarce commodity in my life, something precious to be guarded in the manner the African bushman guards the location of his family's waterhole, passing the secret down to his son.

Our ancestors were more aware by far of the presence—or absence—of water, than we their descendants. The earliest villages and towns were built on riverbanks or near lakes and freshwater springs. A contaminated water supply brought epidemics of typhoid or dysentery, which frequently were followed by death.

My own grandmother had hauled buckets of water from a well to wash her dishes.

Water became a way of life for the adventurous who set out to explore new lands. Some spent years at sea on whaling vessels.

It is restful, when life has been filled with troubles, to disregard those problems for a time and let the mind play with something so common that one seldom gives it any thought: a stone; a beetle; water. That is what I was doing as I let cold water from the hose spray over my bare legs and toes; as I watched it turn into rainbows in the sunlight.

Water. I had never thought about it much before.

We seek contact with water somewhat the way we consciously or unconsciously seek contact with rock. We purchase hot tubs, build swimming pools, sign up for whitewater raft trips, charter fishing boats, enter

63

sailing regattas, spend many of our leisure hours surfing and waterskiing. Even today we are crippled by droughts and polluted streams. We cannot survive without water.

Genesis tells us that water existed when the world still was in chaos: "The earth was without form and void, and darkness was upon the face of the deep; and the Spirit of God was moving over the face of the waters."[10] Before the creation of light, there was water. That truth is inherent in the life of every individual born, too, for a mother's womb is both watery and dark.

Long after birth, my world remained watery. As a tiny child, tucked into my bed under the eaves in a rented cottage on Fire Island, I was lulled to sleep by the muffled boom of the Atlantic surf. I felt at home near lakes and rivers and wandering meadow brooks. From the age of twelve on, I slept in a room "on the water side" of my grandfather's house whenever I spent the summer at Stony Brook. I could raise my shade and look out over Westmeadow Creek and the salt marsh grass, and the beach beyond with its line of summer cottages. Further out rippled the luminous blue water of Long Island Sound.

The Sound was home to me, but the ocean pure mystery. So great was the mystery, the faint outlines of far-off ships penciled on the horizon, the roaring surf glittering like broken glass in the sun, the foam and bits of cork and kelp tossed along the beach, and the seashells I treasured in forgotten pockets, that I later found no difficulty accepting the mythic meaning given to vast bodies of water.

In one's dreams an ocean is symbolic of potentiality. As my creative self became renewed and I could write again, I dreamed of children shouting and laughing, clambering over huge rocks along the shore of a sunlit sea. The dream left me more content than I had been for months. It did not enter my head that this was one way God was speaking to me during a period when words such as *conversion* and *salvation* repelled me.

If we accept the modern interpretation of myth as a poetic, intuitive way of presenting a truth that cannot be expressed clearly in any other way, we understand how bereft we have become. Our scientifically enlightened age discounts the validity of truths expressed imaginatively.

Our need for fantasy and myth is always there; when squelched, they continue to rise again in one form or another. Although we no longer believe we'll fall off the edge of the world if we sail across the ocean, we like to read of fabled cities beneath the sea, and mermaids and water sprites and other beings of the deep. We read of the sea gods of Norsemen and Greek, of floods and storms, and journeys like that of Odysseus. Some of the stories, founded upon historical events, have taken on mythic meaning over a period of centuries.

Rain is practically synonymous with fertility, whereas storms symbolize chaos or anger. Still water denotes peace, but may also symbolize stagnancy. Flowing water—rivers, streams and fountains—depict vitality. Psychologists tell us that a dream of crossing a river often portends a fundamental life change. One thinks immediately of Moses leading the children of Israel across the Red Sea from slavery to freedom, a real-life river crossing that did indeed symbolize a major change. It was followed a long time after by the Israelites crossing over the Jordan into the Promised Land. Centuries later American slaves found a depth of religious meaning in the river symbolism, and sang poignant spirituals about crossing the River Jordan.

I did not dream of crossing a river but a chasm. The experience was so vivid that, to this day, the dream seems real. I was caught in a raging blizzard on a steep mountain slope overlooking a gorge. The only way of escape was a shaky chairlift, the type skiers use. This antiquated lift could hold but one person at a time. My companions insisted I go first since I was the smallest and lightest member of the group. I drew back. I've always been afraid of heights, and so I cried out, "I can't!" Then an inner change occurred and the opposite words came out: "I *can* do it. Yes, I *can!*" I climbed into the lift and sailed out over the chasm to the other side.

The chairlift dream hinted that, no matter how hopeless my external life might seem, something good was happening to me internally.

A simple task, watering the roses, had become an unexpected bridge from the outer world to the inner one. The spiritual significance of water was touching me—water as baptism. To my surprise, I understood now why early converts had been submerged in a river instead of being "sprinkled" at baptism. The rite provided a visceral experience of stepping out into the deep where there was no sure footing anymore, nothing to cling to. All depended on faith. By *acting throuqh* the symbolism, the meaning became clear.

I could understand, too, why the first baptisms took place at dawn when the heavy darkness was fading and the sky brightening with color and light, and why the priest or bishop set his hands upon the shoulders of the baptized one and physically turned his body toward the east.

A person need not go around the world to Lourdes,

or back through history to the pool at Bethsaida, to learn the healing, restorative quality of water. It can happen in a city yard. That is where, tired and overly warm from attempting to cope with a mess of brambles, I realized how thirsty I was. I dealt with the physical thirst by taking a long drink from the hose and letting the water splash over face and hands and shirt. After that, drenched to the skin, I looked honestly at the spiritual drought within my soul.

I could not avoid it any longer. I had lived for twenty-four months without the One who called Himself the Living Water. I had drunk from other wells, but not one of them had quenched my thirst.

VI

Waiting

VI

*Be strong, and let your heart take courage, all you
who wait for the Lord!*

(Psalm 31:24)

Like the Prodigal Son in the parable, I had traveled to
a far country. But there was a major difference. He knew
his way home. I did not.

The one route available I could not bring myself to
take. I might have visited a few churches, selected one,
and started to attend steadily on Sundays. But worshiping in any church would have brought to the surface a

71

flood of unhealed memories. I had not dealt openly with the bitter anger festering in my heart. I continued to avoid traditional forms of Christianity.

It is the prerogative of almighty God to reach us any way He chooses. We may look for Him in the thundering words of a prophet, but He can speak as clearly through a meadow mouse. His way of confronting us unerringly when we least expect Him to do so is His divine signature.

If the proper definition of *angel* is "messenger from God," we are naive to limit the use of the word to those filmy apparitions with wings and halos found in old pictures and Sunday school plays. At times when we cannot be touched by pastor or family members or friends, God is able to employ a total stranger as His messenger, perhaps a grocery clerk or a passenger on a bus, even an author or composer from another century.

I know of no law stating that an angel must be a human figure. In my case, chickadee and tulip, ladybug, cricket and worm may have been His angels watching over me in love.

The silence, too, possessed angelic qualities. It often seemed to be a living presence—and who can say it was not?—a guide leading me back to people and eventually into a community of love. It was the silence that provided a thread of communication between two who long had been strangers—my husband and myself. We scarcely spoke whenever Lindsay stopped by to see the children or to pay bills. One afternoon, however, touched by the troubled expression on his careworn face, I shared the sense of renewal I was finding through silence.

He brightened momentarily and nodded, saying,

"You might care to drop in at the Friends Meeting some Sunday. I bicycled out there once. It was beautiful."

Curious, I followed my husband's suggestion. The meetinghouse of "the quiet Quakers" was so unpretentious that I'd driven down Stark Avenue many times without noticing it. On Sunday mornings there was no ordained pastor in charge, no service, no music; merely a gathering of about thirty people who "centered down" into silence. Any words spoken, and at times there were quite a few, found their source in this great communal silence that, for a newcomer like me, seemed alive.

I returned to the Meeting regularly and came to know people who were refreshingly honest. They did not pretend to believe one thing while practicing another. They believed in peace and they practiced peace, to the point of staunchly refusing to support our country's armed intervention in Vietnam. They believed every part of life is holy, whether or not it can be described in religious vocabulary. Daily they attempted to live out this belief. At the heart of everything they said and did was a basic tenet: there is that of God in every man, even in the hardened criminal and those who are difficult to love.

More than that, the Friends believed it is our responsibility to *seek out* this "divine spark" hidden within each person who comes our way.

They were human. They bickered at times, and sometimes their marriages failed. These shortcomings were not treated lightly. Such matters were handled with discreet counseling (the Quaker expression for it is "eldering"), and loving concern.

The Friends spoke of the Inner Light, a term synonomous to some with "the Christ within." I could center down to the point where my spirit became very still, but the concept of inner light was strange to me yet. Another phrase often used, "waiting upon the Lord," made more sense.

Most of us look at waiting as a time when nothing is happening, the period before things begin to happen. But waiting without hope is quite different from waiting with hope. In the shared silence on Sunday mornings, I learned to hope again. I discovered I was no longer waiting until the healing took place. Instead, the waiting was, in some way I could not define, an integral part of the healing process.

I realized how much my own backyard had taught me about waiting with hope. If I wished to discover what was inside an insect egg, I could not pry it open. I must wait. If I wanted to watch a mother robin's new brood, I must wait. In order to know if my industrious pruning made any difference to the roses . . . I had to wait. The Quaker Meeting simply reinforced a lesson I'd already learned.

A friend once commented that when we are alienated from each other it is because we are living so far from God. I found this to be true. In the shared silence, as I waited for God to come near, I began to draw close to other human beings again. Shyly and slowly, I reached out to make new friends.

These strong and compassionate Quakers surely were part of the heavenly host of angels God sent to surround me and bear me up so that I would not "dash my foot against a stone." Was it coincidence or part of His plan that many of them, due to a keen interest in good stewardship, turned out to be superb gardeners?

The White Queen arbitrarily set the limits of her believing at six impossible things before breakfast. When you turn toward the God of the universe, the impossible things go on forever.

Months passed. Before my eyes, one more impossible thing began to take place. It looked as if Lindsay might be coming home to stay!

He had moved from one job to another trying to earn an adequate living: from grocery clerk to printshop, and then to the systems analysis department at the hospital where he once had been a highly respected chaplain. Presently he was selling Fuller Brush products full-time in one of Portland's loveliest old neighborhoods.

"My room over in northwest Portland is too small to accommodate the big cartons of window spray and jugs of liquid soap," he told me one day. "Do you suppose I could use the spare bedroom over here?"

"Sure," I agreed, not suspecting the absurdity of what was about to happen. Fuller Brush eventually opened up the communication lines between us. Lindsay needed to spend a couple of hours each week sorting and packaging hundreds of scrub brushes, shampoos and other products. Being a door-to-door salesman is not an easy way to earn a living and he seemed relieved when I offered to help with the packaging.

Crosslegged on the spare bedroom floor, we worked and talked. Both of us admitted to one another that life lived separately was not any better than life lived together. Either way, we faced problems. Either way spelled pain. I don't know who raised the question first, but we found ourselves asking: Could two people who had grown so far apart find any common ground on which to build a new relationship? One thing was certain: it would have to be a new marriage. We had grown and changed.

Lindsay's dark hair was turning silvery now. Looking at him one day I felt a pang of tenderness, even as I realized the gulf that had grown up between us.

What would we talk about? Secretly I wondered if a couple who had hurt one another so deeply would be able to form new bonds of trust.

Each of us had read Rollo May's book *Love and Will*.

"We could try it," said Lindsay one day. He was busy screwing the long handle into a sidewalk broom. He set it against the bedroom wall before continuing: "I mean, we could try what Rollo May suggests. Maybe it is possible *to will ourselves to love.*"

I nodded, knowing how tough it would be. It would mean acting as if we loved when, in reality, both of us were numb. It would mean waiting in hope for love to grow, and willing ourselves to love while we waited.

Outside the back door that spring the roses bloomed more profusely than they had for many years. Joyfully I carted buckets full of compost from one side of the yard to the other, spading it carefully around the shrubs. The mint was pushing through the earth in tall green spikes. Near the hose spigot I made a remarkable discovery. There, alongside the foundation of the house where the spigot dripped, was something I had never noticed before: a plant with pale green serrated leaves. A library book identified it as lemon balm. Instead of one kind of tea, I had two growing in my yard!

Lindsay would be coming by for dinner. I went in to brew him a special pot of tea.

I had been reading Blake earlier that afternoon. "The

Four Zoas" contained words that sprang from the page with piercing accuracy:

> *What is the price of Experience? do men buy it*
> *for a song? Or wisdom for a dance in*
> *the street?*
> *No, it is bought with the price of all that a*
> *man hath, his house, his wife, his*
> *children.*[11]

They were heavy words, speaking directly to our condition. Yet the newly discovered sprigs of lemon balm spoke to our condition, too. The leaves were fresh and young and green.

And the earthenware teapot had two cups sitting beside it tonight, instead of one.

VII
The First Garden

VII

Thou crownest the year with thy bounty.
(Psalm 65:11)

It happened. Lindsay did come home. On a hot, early summer afternoon I drove our old red Chevy bus over to his rooming house to help him load up his few meager belongings: books, papers, calligraphy supplies, a couple of old pots and pans, classical guitar. I can recall no feeling of delight, but rather one of shakiness, as I wondered for the hundredth time: Could we actually *decide* to make marriage work? Could we will ourselves into love?

Much of our story is too private to be shared. But with my husband's permission, I will share the words of his that I copied into a commonplace book a year or two after he came home. I take them out to read at least two or three times a year because their freshness has never diminished.

We had been talking of miracles one day and Lindsay said, with a spark of the old fire in his eyes: "Personal and social change, born of miracle, is the gift of forgiveness." He stopped a moment to think about it, then continued: "A miracle is not simply the reversal of natural law. A miracle is the consequence of love taking chances to work change for the sake of the beloved. When love speaks to persons, miracles happen; but there are no miracles without risk. Love can't play it safe. Love takes chances for the sake of the beloved."

These words were the culmination of many months of growing. We had been striving not to accuse one another but to affirm. It was not easy, but then we had not expected it to be. Once, when we were pushing our way doggedly through a particularly difficult day, Lindsay reminded me that "the tedious reality is the counterbalance to the glorious reality."

We were quite poor at the time, with department store credit offices calling to inquire when we expected to be able to pay bills, and the refrigerator shelves looked frighteningly empty.

"It seems to me that we're getting an extra dose of 'tedious reality,'" I grumbled. But I followed the grumbling with a grin. Right outside our back door, I could see a first-rate example of the glorious reality, an honest-to-goodness garden. My first!

The laurel hedge running along the back edge of our property had been trimmed, the rusty swingset given away, blackberry vines and weeds chopped, the sod first broken by spade and then rototilled. In the miniature city yard we had found room for a six-by-nine-foot garden plot with a bit of spare ground at the side for our old dog's swivel chain. Timmy would not have to surrender his place in the sun—not yet, anyway.

Late in the spring my students had brought me extra presents—leeks (which did not grow), rhubarb (which did), and some strange-looking brown bulbs called Jerusalem artichokes.

"Don't throw them away," cautioned the student who gave this gift to me. "You'll love them. Jerusalem artichokes taste like water chestnuts. And you know how expensive *they* are."

"I've planted snow peas," I informed my family at dinner, "and swiss chard, and cukes, and carrots, radishes, green onions, lettuce, and six tomato plants, too. Oh yes, and a few pumpkin seeds for jack o'lanterns in the fall; and a small patch of corn."

"All that in our yard?" asked Lindsay with an incredulous look in his eye.

"Some of it may not grow," I murmured. "I know so little about gardening. But think of the money we'll save if some of it does grow. I'm doing everything organically, by the way. No bug sprays, understand? I happen to *like* bugs."

He stared at me with amusement and a shade of doubt.

Every conceivable spot was filled with vegetables or flowers. Friends from the Meeting who gardened organically passed on the information that nasturtiums repel aphids and other insects; marigolds banish the tiny threadlike nematodes so detrimental to tomatoes; blue borage contributes some mysterious element that helps other plants to flourish.

By early summer the plot had turned into a palette of color spilling all over the place: gold, red, green and blue, with a few delicate lavender and white blossoms mixed among the brighter hues.

An organic gardener soon learns that not every insect or bug is an enemy. Many have proved to be extremely beneficial to a garden. Heading the list in my notebook were the ladybugs, which consumed aphids by the thousand, and also a large black beetle I might have destroyed in other years. That beetle and his cousins, much to my amazement, ate slugs.

As for the slugs, I tried every known remedy, including pans of beer, an expensive idea after the first week or so. Finally I invented a new solution. I gave them their own special stuff to eat: wilted cabbage leaves, carrot peelings, onion skins and grapefruit rinds. Thereafter they feasted contentedly and left silvery trails throughout the vegetable patch, harming few "legitimate" crops.

"Have you gone mad?" a neighbor demanded one day. "Feeding *slugs?*"

The secret, of course, was that once they'd gathered around their dinner piles set in various spots in the garden, it was easy to dispose of them. But always I stopped first to think of Chardin's idea of interconnectedness, and to wonder exactly how the slugs of the world might be rooted in cosmos. Was it only that they provided excellent, vitamin-filled meals for ducks and snakes and toads? Or was there another answer?

I put in surprisingly few hours of work on that garden. Why do a lot of work if the garden was able to take care of itself? I dug out dandelions here and there because their roots gobbled up nutrients and seemed to add no necessary ingredient to the soil. I filled kettles with peapods and lettuce and corn to prepare for our evening meal.

But why, for instance, pull up nettles just because other people labeled the nettle a weed? I knew it was feeding the plants growing close to it. The American Indians, centuries ago, had learned the value of weeds and left many of them growing among their vegetables.

Most of the time, when the family thought I was working, I was out there squatting on my heels to watch things happen. In the garden I reverted to the invaluable habit formed in childhood. I "did my thinking."

I suppose it could have been called a rambling sort of meditation. Because I spent hours leaning on my hoe instead of using it, absorbed in the fascinating life unfolding at my feet, the garden came to be known as my Study Garden. Instead of laboring in it, I studied it.

Daily it astonished me to think of how oblivious we've become to the abundance of God's creation. Our youngsters clamor for shoes that we cannot afford, the telephone bill skyrockets, the toilet floods, and the plumber must be called. So great are these anxieties that we are apt to miss the wealth being offered to us.

Everything in my garden grew so wild and free that it soon became a garden without rows. One of the prettiest weeds, a sturdy plant with dark green leaves, had appeared in several different locations.

"See if you can tell me what it is," I begged Lindsay. "It isn't listed in my weed book."

He left his science fiction paperback open on the coffeetable and disappeared. In a few minutes I heard him laughing.

"It isn't in your weed book for a good reason," he told me. "It isn't a weed. Those are your potato plants."

"They can't be," I protested. "I didn't set out any potatoes."

Nevertheless, he was right. Potato plants had grown from some of the thickest peelings I had buried months ago! In the fall we would collect a full bucket of potatoes, several large bakers and many smaller ones to boil and mash.

I had mulched heavily with rotted hay from a farm, adding sloppy piles of mown grass, chopped weeds and other debris. Occasionally, reaching beneath the mulch to test the dampness of the soil, I found a surprise. Once it was a vegetable or fruit resembling a baby watermelon. On closer scrutiny, I realized it was only a cucumber left by mistake to grow on and on . . . and on.

By August, the pumpkin vine had strayed across the yard, back to the hedge, and up the side of the garage. The vine contained four large green globes that gradually turned gold as the summer waned. The tomato plants bowed under the weight of ripening fruit. We were waiting impatiently for the corn to ripen so that we could pop it out of the garden and into a pot of boiling water. But our dog was waiting for something else.

Timmy was the only family member dismayed by the garden. The runaway vines and plants had taken over every bit of his part of the yard. The old mutt lay on the back porch, his head on his golden paws, reminiscing about better days when he had been able to bark at bees and nip the heels of any cat who dared to shortcut through his territory.

In gardening, as in the rest of my life, I had adopted a new watchword: Be open. The seed of this idea may have been sown in my mind years earlier when I asked my mother to tell me about *her* mother, my dead grand-mother.

"Everyone adored her," said my mother. "Your granny was the kind of person who never said no to anyone if she could possibly say yes."

Through the years, my own outlook had become petrified; things should be done this way or that way, and that was that. If people did not behave as I'd been taught they should behave (because the Bible or the Church said so), they were wrong.

That is a small, closed view. The shattering of my life had broken it and exposed it for what it was: pharisaical. And suddenly the judgmental words, the *shoulds* and *shouldn'ts* and *oughts* and *ought nots* vanished from my vocabulary.

Be open, I told myself constantly. Be open. Say yes to life and marriage and faith. With all your heart and mind, say yes.

It didn't mean I couldn't say no. But I was saying it less frequently and, whenever I did, it was for a firm, good reason, not because of habit.

The openness was reflected in the opulence of the Study Garden. I was willing to try new ideas.

My favorite time to water was mid-evening when the dusk deepened and the stars were appearing one by one. I could hear children playing games, and the cheep of a bird settling down for the night, and sometimes the voices of neighbors talking on their porches. Other than that, the world was still. Lost in thought, I felt trans-ported into another garden altogether, a garden of memories thriving on interior soil.

The popular term "inner healing" refers to the heal-ing of painful memories, many of which are beyond the reach of the conscious mind. We forget we are able to draw real strength from other memories, the ones that bring smiles instead of tears.

I believe the latter kind of healing happened to me during the years I was groping my way out of the darkness. The Bible verses drifting to the surface brought back secure circumstances and mellow times, when a mother and father sat by a bedside reading to two little girls: the stories of Abraham and Joseph, Ruth and Mary and Martha and Jesus.

Something as simple as a pumpkin pie cooling on a kitchen counter, the smell of snow, the first trillium in the spring, can stir fleeting images of another time, images woven inextricably into the person called Mary or Robert or Joe. These images bear with them a sense of renewal and joy. They have the power to heal.

I experienced the validity of this statement when I took a loaf of homemade bread to a nursing home, along with some butter and a jar of currant jelly. The staff allowed even those on restricted diets to share the treat because the healing memories conjured up by homemade bread and butter were worth more than the rigid observance of a special diet.

One resident, who until now had talked only of her aches and pains, spoke of the days she had churned her family's supply of butter, kneaded the bread, carried the milkpails to the dairy in town where it would be sold.

An old man described walking three miles to school in a snowstorm, his lunchpail full of bread-and-butter sandwiches.

Another resident recited the very recipe her mother had used for sourdough biscuits. That afternoon not one mention was made of pain!

Clinging to memories and wishing one could go back

to relive the former times in one's life is not the same as gazing at those warm experiences openly, as a nosegay from an old-fashioned flower garden. Clinging causes pain; the nosegay from this other interior garden bears only the joy one knows when one has been able to move beyond the pain.

When the Study Garden bloomed crazily and randomly in every corner of the yard, the abundance God had bestowed upon us could not be ignored. And that was only the beginning. We were to reap, in the years ahead, a harvest of blessings that not one of us could have foretold.

In Lindsay's words: "When love speaks to persons, miracles happen; but there are no miracles without risk. Love can't play it safe. Love takes chances for the sake of the beloved."

I used to reread those words with my husband in mind, but one day, recognizing their deeper meaning, I went back to my commonplace book and rewrote the passage capitalizing the word *Love*. All this time, a loving heavenly Father had refused to play it safe as He watched over the lives of two of His children. He had taken a great risk and let us go. And now a miracle was happening.

VIII
Trees

For there is hope for a tree,
  if it be cut down, that it will sprout again,
  and that its shoots will not cease.
Though its root grow old in the earth
  and its stump die in the ground,
Yet at the scent of water it will bud
  and put forth branches like a young plant.
                                    (Job 14:7-9)

When we bought our house on 14th Street, there were no trees on our lot. I missed them. I had grown up on a street lined with stately elms and maples. Each spring their branches arched overhead in a green canopy. In the autumn, street gutters were piled with gold and russet leaves.

I was glad, therefore, when the city fathers of Portland embarked on a beautification project and presented families with young trees to plant throughout various neighborhoods.

The year my son arrived home from school with the birdfeeder, another tree, a mountain ash, had been transplanted from a friend's yard to a spot outside my kitchen window.

By the time my husband and I were starting a new life together, this small tree had begun to shoot upward. Birds flocked to its branches to watch me fill the feeder. And so it became "the bird tree."

The mountain ash proved sturdier than it looked. No wind shook it loose from the soil, although our windows sometimes rattled, and a shingle or two blew off the roof. An ice storm crippled the city but, other than bowing under its burden of frozen water, the young tree remained unscathed.

Underground, where they could not be seen, our roots were growing, too, enabling new shoots to spring up around the stump of an old and worn-out marriage. At times any growth in a relationship seems imperceptible. But, like the mountain ash, our marriage held: for one year, then two, and on into the third.

The sheer complexity of a tree captured my imagination. I read that trees depend on the finest and most delicate of root hairs, minute threads lasting usually only a few days or months. Water, bearing valuable mineral nutrients, is drawn into the tree through a labyrinth of roots, and the roots of some trees go down as much as thirty feet!

The structure of leaves is, to me, even more wonderful than a root system. In *This Is a Leaf*, Ross Hutchins tells of the complex design of a leaf. Leaves actually breathe through tiny pores called *stomates*. Through the gap between two kidney-shaped cells of each stomate, air enters the leaf. By a process of transpiration, water is lifted into the air as vapor. According to Hutchins, one square inch of a single apple leaf may have a quarter of a million stomates.

The two kidney-shaped cells of a stomate are called guard cells. These cells govern the amount of moisture entering a leaf by opening and closing the gap between them. Light, combined with the chemical processes going on inside a leaf, helps this to take place.

Scientists give us the mind-boggling estimate that a tree must give off from 200 to 500 pounds of water in order to produce one pound of wood. In addition to the evaporation already described, water escapes into the air as liquid through special water stomates that remain open all the time.

When I sat in the Quaker Meeting on a spring Sunday, my mind wandered to the small tree growing at the side of our house. How extraordinarily intricate it was! Suddenly I knew without a doubt that the One who cared for me enough to give me, first, a silence all my own, and then to lead me into the great healing silence I shared with Friends, was One who cared for every bit of His creation—even our slender mountain ash.

At this point I could also say that I believed in a Creator who inspired wonder.

Where had the wonder gone? Children naturally greet

each dawn with exuberance. Some are more curious, more visceral in their approach than others. As a child I talked to a daddy longlegs by the hour and wished on lucky stones encircled with white rings. After reading about Indians paddling down a river in birchbark canoes, I pounded strips of birchbark with my brother's wooden mallet, determined to make at least a doll-sized canoe. With my birthday pocket knife, I carved the tough end of a seagull feather into a quill pen. And, after that, I soaked rags in a coffee can of water behind the garage, certain they would melt eventually into real paper. I kept hermit crabs as pets, collected bags full of acorns to feed the squirrels each winter, and dreamed of living in a tree.

At the Friends Meeting and during moments spent at the kitchen window looking out at the sparrows and chickadees in the mountain ash, those lost pleasures came back to me as memories awakened; and I began to regain a sense of wonder.

Is it the daily tedium of life that squelches wonder? I am one of many who set this basic human response aside. I am not referring here to sporadic bursts of awe, but to the way we relate on a daily basis to the creation around us.

Is there anything more wonderful than a tree? We walk down an avenue hardly noticing the trees lining the pavement, whereas primitive people would have quite a different reaction. Early tribes, for instance, believed their forests to be haunted by demonic spirits. Ancient Persians were terrified of a forest demon named Siltim, believing he could inflict terrible injury. Malayans, threatened by the invisible Voice Folk, repeated incantations before going into the forest alone.

From Japan and Australia, India and New Guinea, to the continent of Europe, legends of tree spirits are told.

We read of the Tree Women of the Tyrol with enormous gaping mouths and hairy bodies; and the scary Moss Women of Germany with knotty, rootlike feet and lichen hair. Far away, deep in the Central American forests, we come upon the story of the strange bird-headed woman, an exquisite creature able to lure men to death with her beautiful voice.

Not every tree creature was dreaded. One Roumanian sprite, Numa Padura, supposedly helped find children lost in the woods. Most of us have read delightful tales of fairies and elves and stories about the mischievous Greek goatherder-god, Pan.

Often single trees or entire groves were held sacred. The most famous stories involve the Druids, ancient priests of France and Britain and Ireland.

These are more than amusing or frightening tales. They reveal how diligently our ancestors reached, in primitive ways, toward truths that constantly eluded them; and how keenly they sensed their own relationship to the universe.

We cannot return to a primitive way of life, nor would we want to do so. But does this mean our sense of wonder is forever lost? I think not. Brilliant physicists, marine biologists, naturalists, doctors doing research or delivering babies, are filled with wonder much of the time.

As for the rest of us who feel trapped in mundane lives, something as simple and, paradoxically, as complex as a tree can awaken that forgotten response.

Perhaps stress and hurry simply mask our ability to

wonder, in the manner that chlorophyll masks the yellow colors in a leaf.

In leaves, apparently, the pigments exanthophyll and carotene (yellow and orange or red) are always present. At the end of the summer when growth slows and chlorophyll disapppears, these other brilliant pigments show up. The brighter scarlet hues, however, the antho-cyanins, do not appear within the leaf until the coming of autumn.

So does a human life live through its various seasons. I wondered if, in my case, the monotonous "daily color" of my life had come to a standstill at the end of a season and thus had unmasked the red and the gold, the rainbow hues of childhood.

This unmasking requires a death, a renunciation: for the tree the renunciation of chlorophyll, a chemical that has fulfilled its purpose. For myself or any other human being, the renunciation is that of a stable way of life, one that has grown stale and useless. Only then may we risk another season.

My husband and I must be willing to survive many winter seasons. Only by braving our way resolutely through the barren, leafless time could we come again to spring. As a gardener, I no longer dreaded winter. I knew that, beneath the frozen ground, new life stirred.

One evening as I watered the garden, the deeper truth of a favorite Bible passage came to mind. It was the tale of another tree in another garden long ago at the creation of the world. When I closed my eyes, I could hear my mother's voice reading it as my sister and I lay in our beds, side by side, waiting for sleep to come.

God, you will remember, trusted man with the care of plants and trees, the birds and fish and mammals and creeping things in the Garden of Eden. The phrase I loved as a child was "to have dominion over." One thing, however, man and woman did not have dominion over. That was the tree of the knowledge of good and evil, a tree bearing tempting and edible fruit.

What did the memory of that story say to me? I must stop trying to control situations I had no dominion over—my husband's life, for instance, and my children's likes and dislikes. My major responsibility was to be a good steward of the gifts the Creator had given to *me*, not to others. The need to control had been limiting; but, happily, the newly awakened sense of wonder seemed to be opening a door to growth.

IX
Small Things

IX

Four things on earth are small,
  but they are exceedingly wise:
the ants are a people not strong,
  yet they provide their food in the summer;
the badgers are a people not mighty,
  yet they make their homes in the rocks;
the locusts have no king,
  yet all of them march in rank;
the lizard you can take in your hands,
  yet it is in kings' palaces.

(Proverbs 30:24-28)

LET THE EARTH BRING FORTH

When vacations became an impossibility for several years (nine years!), I felt caged, and sometimes filled with despair. Gradually I developed four small ways to move out of despondency.

The first was to reread and savour a bit of Thoreau I'd copied as a young woman: "If I were confined to a corner of a garret all my days like a spider, the world would be just as large to me while I had my thoughts about me."[12]

Thoreau's words are true. When our physical bodies are cramped, our thoughts do not have to be bound in any way. Most of us can get enough physical exercise by gardening, or tramping around a city, or riding a bicycle.

But thoughts, enriched by reading, can help relieve our craving for a change of environment. Thoughts have the power to plunge us into imaginary worlds. In an instant, frayed carpets and dusty corners vanish and we are far away.

My second "way out" was through writing. For others, music or painting or working in clay may offer the opportunity for an interior journey; for me it was putting words on paper. Sometimes I concentrated on a story or poem. More often than not, I poured my heart out on the lined pages of my journal.

The third way came to me in a flash one afternoon when I had climbed the attic stairs to hunt for an old magazine. This attic had been the special domain of our three sons. Now only one of them inhabited it.

With magazine in hand, I lay down on the spare bed at the end of the attic and, for a moment, gazed out the window. Astonished, I realized I had lived in our house for eight years without ever looking through this particular bedroom window. On a rare occasion, I had hurried up the stairs to peek at a strange cloud or something else a son had wanted to show me. But I had no memory of actually *looking through* the narrow window with an intention of observing the panorama stretched before me.

Individual skyscrapers loomed, including the recently built Lloyd Tower. I saw not one but two bridges: the old Steel Bridge, blackened but sturdy, and the brand-new Fremont Bridge cutting like a modernistic arc from one side of the Willamette River to the other. Close at hand, I could see roofs and chimneys, slate-gray and red.

I'd never had an opportunity, until now, to look over the laurel hedge bordering our backyard, and down into the yard of the home behind it. Beyond the roofs and treetops and beyond the office buildings gleaming in late-afternoon sun, I saw the West Hills dotted with miniature houses.

A search soon uncovered at least four other unused windows. In my own house! I had wandered by the window on the stair landing hundreds of times without more than a cursory glance through it. And for years the window in our large walk-in bedroom closet had been hidden by a broken venetian blind. Intrigued, I lifted the blind and stared out. From this viewpoint the street looked different, and more interesting, somehow.

Later, I found a high window in my study closet downstairs. It too had been covered by a shade. Composed of four small panes, the fourth window was set into the side door of our basement. From it I could get an excellent view of ground-feeding birds. I would no longer have to kneel on a kitchen stool to watch them.

This pastime need not be limited to those who dwell

in houses. By varying it slightly, apartment residents may seek out a fresh picture of an overly familiar world. One can look out of *any* window at an unusual time of day—3 a.m., perhaps, or 11 p.m.

Our view may also be enlarged simply by developing a different manner of looking. Grace, a fragile, tiny woman confined to her bed by crippling arthritis, possessed a dauntless spirit. Once when I visited, her eyes lit up and she murmured, "I've been watching that bumblebee on my sill."

Some days it would be nothing more than a cloud or a gust of wind shaking the treetops. From her vantage point (she could not even raise herself on an elbow), she was unable to see the sidewalk, only rooftops and trees and sky. But that one bedroom window enlarged her cramped world.

Thoreau wrote succinctly in a journal entry: "I milk the sky and the earth."[13] That is what my friend Grace had learned to do.

My fourth way of release turned out to be the best, yet also extremely simple. It was to go into my tangled garden and spend several hours observing the hidden universe. Our lawn never had been well-manicured; nor could we afford loads of expensive barkdust to treat our flowerbeds each spring. The garden continued to be a jungle of vegetables, weeds, herbs and flowers. Every inch of it, however, disclosed thrilling secrets. They unfolded themselves to me one by one, as I learned to scout for them.

The yard had become a foreign country to explore. Each season offered new gifts and, with the gifts, further questions. What insect had deposited the clusters of orange eggs on the backs of several leaves? And the elongated white ones, and those that were pale yellow and slightly larger than the rest?

When I felt as if nothing exciting or new would ever happen to me again, I fled to the yard and deliberately became absorbed in its life. If I watched quietly, I might be lucky and come upon some ants milking their herds of "cows." At times several ants took turns milking the same aphid, or ant-cow, much to my amusement.

The black field cricket nibbling its dinner so daintily— what contortions it went through a little later when it made its toilet!

Two hours in the yard brought refreshment. Perhaps society would be faced with less delinquency if children from the toddler stage on were taught to take delight in the dramas enacted at their feet, the curious things happening in sidewalk cracks, weed patches, empty lots, yards and meadows. Enchanted by their environment, they might be less inclined to destroy it.

Green things growing held as much interest for me as the life cycles of spiders and aphids and ants.

I counted every single shrub and weed and flower, every growing thing to be found on our lot, front and back, over the months. This project lasted several seasons and required countless trips to the library. I finally listed 63 varieties, three of which I could not name after extensive research. One weed bore a miniscule lavender flower. I asked lifelong gardeners and hunted through books but never did identify it.

No two springs or summers turned out to be the same. Biographers writing of Darwin tell us he spent 40 years studying earthworms. Were I to continue studying all that grew or lived on our lot, I would not be finished in two hundred years!

This may sound idyllic. It was not. Lindsay and I struggled. Most of the time we felt physically weary and emotionally drained, anxious about unpaid bills. But we were surviving. Just as garden soil needs replenishing, so does the soil of marriage. Together we were building new soil.

The new little steps we were taking together and separately, and the new things we talked about, shared, explored, could be compared to the garbage I still chopped daily and buried in the heap. It was compost of a different sort, and would be transformed into marriage soil.

Meanwhile, both of us had become members of the Friends Meeting. At the dinner table, instead of commiserating about family problems, we spoke of what had transpired during the day in our separate lives: the new book I was writing, the sign painting career my husband had finally launched into instead of selling Fuller Brush products and carpets and insurance. Now that he was combining his artistic skills and sense of design with his manual dexterity, he felt better about himself. He had grown a beard again, flecked with silver like his hair. I thought he looked distinguished, even in the soft, old blue denim shirts he wore while painting signs.

Creative endeavors—his sign painting business and my writing and teaching—made excellent soil for our growing relationship.

The garden itself became "marriage soil." My husband did not learn to like gardening, but he thoroughly enjoyed my excitement over each crop. He boasted about the size of the tomatoes, the delicious flavor of the first corn.

A great sadness remained within us. We'd lost much

SMALL THINGS

that could never be retrieved, and building a relationship to take its place was like tree-growing, a very slow
process.

As I had learned to look at familiar scenes through
seldom used windows, so did we learn to look at the
world about us and at one another with different eyes.

We tried to accept and love one another the way we
were, instead of the way each of us wanted the other to
be. We tried to stop and *listen* to what was being said, to
say "thank you" for little things instead of ignoring
them entirely. Long before my husband could bring
himself to say "I love you" again, he said it without
words by having a kettle of homemade soup simmering
on the back of the range when I arrived home from a day
at the library; by lettering silly bits of graffiti in elaborate
calligraphy to make me laugh when I felt like dissolving
in tears; by inventing unheard-of casserole combina-
tions with the same old supply of brown rice and left-
overs; by raving over my homemade bread, not once
but every single time I baked it.

As a matter of fact, looking back, I cannot name the
day he finally said, "I love you," and yet he says it now
to me, sometimes several times a day.

Over a period of time the pain diminished. Growth
cannot take place *without* pain, but the pain of growth,
whether shared or experienced alone, is qualitatively
different from the wretched, gnawing misery caused by
selfishness and hatred in two lives.

We floundered, still in darkness. But this, too, was
qualitatively different from the darkness that had mani-
fested itself previously during my years alone when I
had been cut off from love.

X

The Other Side of Darkness

The earth was without form and void, and
darkness was upon the face of the deep.

(Genesis 1:2)

How was this darkness different? The earlier experience had been a darkness of death. Everything I held dear to me had disappeared.

In such a threatening darkness, fearful spirits lie ready to torment us at every turn. It is the black, scary forest in fairy tales—in "Hansel and Gretel," for instance. It is Dante's dark wood and Milton's hell. It is the

Underworld described vividly by the Roman poet Vergil. Here Cerebus, the three-headed guard dog, watches over the juncture of two of the five rivers separating the world above from the world below. Here, too, is Charon, the ancient boatman, ready to carry across those souls buried with proper passage money.

When we are spiritually bankrupt, as I was at one time, we do not have the passage money to traverse this darkness.

Our tendency is to be afraid of the dark. Primitive people, especially, feared the mystery of darkness and the terrors it held. They dreaded the coming of night, the gloomy months of winter, the unknown darkness-after-death. Once the sun vanished, who could be certain it would return?

The imagery of darkness, aptly used for the world of the dead, is prominent also in mythic tales of pre-birth. Some believed light existed first, or at least that it coexisted with the dark. In China, Yang—the male principle—symbolizes light; Yin—the female principle—symbolizes darkness.

One Scandinavian story tells of an enormous abyss full of magic power. To the south was nothing but blazing heat, and to the north only freezing darkness. Life leaped into being when the opposites met within the abyss. Sparks from the south combined with ice crystals from the north.

Another piece of writing, the *Prose Edda*, depicted the opposite: night was the mother of day. This is the way it is seen in most ancient tales. Jews, Arabs, Celts and Germanic people, among others, believed the new day began at sundown.

We rarely experience true, complete darkness anymore. Used to flicking switches to obtain instant light, we are estranged from the darkness, even though it is meshed with the very stuff of life. Our estrangement from physical darkness well may point to our separation from the dark side of ourselves.

I needed to find a way to handle the darkness within myself and others, and so it was that myths and the writings of Carl Jung filled the gap for the time being. Jung maintains we each carry a shadow made up of this dark side of ourselves, often consisting of our negative traits, the ones we try to hide.

Mythic symbol and story provide valuable ways to recognize the shadow side of personality so that we no longer repress it. Dreams serve this function, too.

No wonder dreams and visions have played an important role in man's earthly pilgrimage! They present us with vital information about our hidden selves, and about the divine. Dreams are one of the beautiful legacies given to us by darkness, a birthright we are far too inclined to toss aside.

While I was alone, a friend presented me with a copy of *The Dark Night of the Soul* by St. John of the Cross. Had I read it then instead of years later, I might have understood that the first darkness of which I write is a common experience. But I do not know if I would have had the moral courage to journey through that darkness, trusting God would be with me in the very hour I thought Him gone forever.

Neither physical nor spiritual darkness is always frightening. As healing started to take place, an almost palpable darkness wrapped around me like a blanket. The physical darkness felt friendly, too. In the evening, after I had watered the garden, I would sit on the back steps watching daylight fade.

Slowly the night enveloped me until at last I could

hardly see my coffee mug or the handful of zinnias I had picked. I cannot say I experienced true dark. The shadowy rooftops and chimneys remained visible; the bare outline of the garbage can was there. But at least I was sitting still to acknowledge the passage of day into night.

Gradually streetlights flared on, and the lights in homes. The moon rose overhead in the inky sky. Stars began to glitter.

On summer nights the neighborhood children stayed out long past their usual bedtime to play hide-and-seek. I recorded the warmth of this child-filled darkness in my journal:

Calling to Children on a Summer Night

Night's dark gravy
Pours over the city,
Blotting the pure gold
Tree-chained nine o'clock sky.

I call
To the racket hidden
In yards and porches.

My heart's ear listens
While in the tremulous dark
Each solid thing, each trunk,
Each step and brick and stoop . . .
And every marigold
Is bounced with laughter.

In times of rest, the natural rhythm of life presses upon us and we find ourselves surprisingly in time with the beat. When it happened to me, I no longer worried about being out-of-step with other human beings. I *wanted* to slough off trivialities, to find time to think and create; time to *be*.

According to the Bhagavad-Gita, "The world is imprisoned in its own activity, except when actions are performed as worship of God."[14]

"Life is meant to be lived from a Center, a divine Center," wrote the twentieth-century Quaker Thomas Kelly. "There is a divine Abyss within us all, a holy Infinite Center, a Heart, a Life who speaks to us and through us to the world. We have all heard this holy whisper at times. . . ."[15]

Without being fully aware of it, I had passed from the darkness of death to the darkness of birth. Before birth, a human embryo must live a certain length of time without light in the womb. Without this stage, growth would be impossible. Many life forms, in fact, need a world of almost total darkness. The life cycle of some creatures is dependent upon the seasonal variations of light and darkness, in addition to variations in temperature.

And so in the garden I was surrounded by other darknesses besides that of night: the darkness within the seed, and inside of eggs and cocoons; and the great seething darkness of the compost heap where decay became a door into life.

Darkness without; darkness within. In the outer darkness I heard the laughter of children. But my heart's ear was listening to what Thomas Kelly had termed "a holy whisper."

XI

Light

*Let us then cast off the works of darkness and put
on the armor of light.*

(Romans 13:12)

"You are ready," the holy whisper prompted. "It is
time to leave the womb of darkness."

I cannot recall the exact day I stood in the middle of
the garden exclaiming, "The light is everywhere!"

There may have been a sudden change in weather. In
our part of the country, after a period of wet, gloomy
days, sunlight breaking through a putty-colored sky

can be dazzling. Washed with gold, tree trunks, leaves, flowers, lawns, rocks, even the sides of houses glisten.

Streaming through the leaded tulip windows at the front of our house, it splashed in rainbows on the living room floor. The white woodwork took on a mellow glow.

Physicists tell us light has the properties of both waves and particles. It travels at the awesome speed of 186,000 miles a second. Without it, everything in the world would look black, because the color of any given object depends on which light rays bounce off it and which are absorbed. We are beginning to understand how birds, and many insects, too, use the sun as a compass to guide them in traveling great distances, often thousands of miles.

It has been calculated that more than 130 million million tons of matter are converted yearly by the sun into energy and this is the source of our sunshine.

Is it possible to picture 130 million million tons?

Marine biologists describe the "living light" given off by luminescent creatures far beneath the sea, the same "cool" light we recognize in fireflies and glowworms and in certain types of minerals.

We have invented matches, artificial light, laser surgery techniques, nuclear fuel, and terrifying nuclear bombs. We know ways to heat our modern buildings with solar energy. But mathematical equations, chemical formulas, painstaking experiments and advanced technology convince most of us that the more we know about light, the less sure we can be of *what* we know.

To some extent, we have harnessed light to serve our needs. But it has never been tamed. When fire sweeps through a national forest destroying acres of trees, when sunlight scorches our farmland or blisters our skin, it commands our respect.

Early in the spring when the days lighten and daffodils bloom, something stirs within us—a longing, a cry unheard, a desire to realize once again our *connectedness* to earth and sea and sky; a vague remembrance that we are, as Chardin said, *enkekosmismene*. The drawing power of the sun reminds us that we too are part of the universe.

When we remember that life would be nonexistent without light, we can understand why so many of the early religions were devoted to worship of the sun god.

Stone Age people painted different kinds of sun circles on the walls of caves. Thousands of years ago, when it was believed that the sun traveled around the earth, the swastika symbol represented the sun and its moving rays. Throughout the world the design has been discovered on pottery, coins, jewelry and walls.

The Sumerians, an early Mesopotamian culture, worshiped the sun god Shamesh, telling stories of how he was driven high into the sky every day. One wheel of his chariot was thought to be a flaming disk, and this is what people saw as the sun. Shamesh started his journey from the Mountain of the East. At dusk his chariot drove through the door of the Mountain of the West where he journeyed beneath the ground throughout the night.

The Egyptian sun god, Ra, had many names and shapes. He could be a disk, a hawk, a beetle, a phoenix, a lion and a cat. At daybreak he was known as Horus; at midday, Ra; and throughout the night when he fought wicked serpents, his name was Osiris.

Story after beautiful story is told. The Greek poet

Ovid relates the tale of Phaethon, the mortal son of the great sun god, Helios. Foolishly, Helios promised to grant Phaethon the dearest wish of his heart, and then regretted it. The boy asked to drive his father's golden chariot across the sky, a feat no mortal was strong enough to accomplish. When the wish had been granted, the young charioteer ended up careening into the river, but not until the entire world had caught on fire. What a splendid description of a sunset this is!

We could wander for days through Oriental and Persian and Indian myths of light; through books telling of monuments and temples honoring light . . . the obelisks, the Sphinx, and Stonehenge, that strange and wonderful formation of rocks on English soil. On the first day of the spring equinox, the shadow of the sun falls across the great stone altar, seeming to show that this must have been a place where people gathered to worship light. It is thought, too, that the great rocks were used to make astronomical calculations about eclipses of the sun and the moon.

Imagery of light frequently symbolizes the beautiful and the good. I have written of internal and external silence, and of two kinds of dark. After I had spent years in spiritual darkness, I believe God led me to rest a while in my sunlit garden—just physically to rest—in order to prepare me for the dazzling of His inner light.

He had used this method constantly to guide me. For five years I stubbornly had refused to open the Bible and read the eloquent, simple stories with their symbols of earth, seed, root, tree, leaf, water, darkness and light. And so God led me unsuspectingly *to live the parables* through my garden instead. Only the Lord of the universe could use so ingeniously a narrow, rather shabby city yard!

At last the holy whisper breathed, "Now!" The divine abyss cracked open. I was in the Light.

To be semantically correct, I suppose I should say, "The Light was in me," but that is not the way I experienced it. I felt as if time had disappeared and the Light shone within and without. "The light is everywhere!" I'd exclaimed in the garden a month or two before this experience of inner Light came to pass.

Mystics and poets have groped for words to describe it. St. Francis wrote a Hymn to Light and, at the end of his *Divine Comedy,* Dante cries:

> So now a living light
>   encompassed me:
> In veil so luminous I was
>   enwrapt
> That naught, swathed in such
>   glory, could I see.[16]

He goes on to describe a blazing river of light with iridescent flowers growing along either side of it.

The journals of George Fox and other Quakers indicate they were steeped in this light. Kelly calls it the inward Living Christ, the Shekinah of the soul. The Friends with whom Lindsay and I fellowshiped each Sunday at the Meeting House on Stark Street centered their lives in it and were energized by its power.

But more than any other descriptions of light, long-forgotten passages from the Bible drifted through my mind: the one from John where Jesus states so clearly, "I am the light of the world . . .",[17] and the haunting words, "The light shines in the darkness, and *the darkness has not overcome it,*"[18] and the picture of the heavenly city in the book of Revelation, a city that needs no sun or moon because "the glory of God is its light."[19]

One cannot remain in the light continually. One must go on working, preparing meals, spading and weeding the garden. But I discovered how to take a few minutes *while* I worked to grow still and let the inner Light invade my being.

I knew I must not stop here. Life in the garden could not remain static and neither could I. I must go on. Home was somewhere. I had not caught sight of it yet; but, like a migrating bird, I was guided by an inner compass now.

XII
Another Garden

*And you shall be like a watered garden, like a
spring of water, whose waters fail not.*

(Isaiah 58:11)

One season melted into another. Once again I grew a
garden, different from the first, different from the second or third. Gardens are never the same. This time I
tried beets that didn't grow, and onions that did. Instead of pumpkins, we harvested enough zucchini to
feed the whole neighborhood.

There was darkness. And light.

I felt restless, spiritually hungry, but I did not know why. I could not name what was missing from my life. I suspected Lindsay felt that way sometimes, too, although on the surface everything seemed smooth.

A year before, when he was still a door-to-door salesman, he had made a friend. The customer turned out to be an Episcopal clergyman who had come to Oregon several years after we had left the church. Herb and Lindsay chatted over coffee that day. Before Lindsay headed home, Herb said: "I'd like to see you back on the team."

"The children on the school playground think I'm strange," I laughed when Lindsay drove up shortly thereafter and parked the car. I wiped the sweat from my forehead. "I guess they've never seen a mother in tennis shoes lugging big plastic garbage sacks of leaves home to dump on her garden." I waved my hand at the seven bulging bags I'd set against the side of the house. "Maple leaves are pure gold, you know; they make an excellent mulch."

He hadn't heard a word of my garden chatter. His eyes told me his mind had traveled far away. Later, over a cup of tea, he repeated Herb's comment, adding, "I don't know what got into me. Nobody had said that to me before. You and I left that stuff behind us years ago, Mary, but I cried all the way home."

I patted his shoulder, not knowing what to say.

Neither of us mentioned the incident again. I knew in my heart that we could not grow backwards into something that had once been real for us, yet my heart ached whenever I thought of the loss.

Months later, my husband came into the kitchen with a handful of mail. "We've been invited to Gene's ordination," he said quietly. "He was such a faithful member of our congregation in Salem that . . . well, I'd like to go."

We had not been inside a church for five years. We were in for a surprise. We were not the only ones who had changed. The Church had, too! The prayer book liturgy was in the process of being revised, and we felt a new warmth, an excitement and a vitality that had not been there before. During the Communion service, when the bishop said, with fervor, "The peace of the Lord be always with you," people suddenly got up and moved up and down the aisles greeting one another joyously.

"My, but it's good to see both of you!" an old friend exclaimed, hugging each of us right in the middle of the service.

We were in the chapel at Good Samaritan Hospital where my husband had served as chaplain. When the time came to receive Communion, I followed Lindsay up to the altar rail.

We did not say much to one another that evening. A party followed the ordination, with plenty of food and laughter and conversation. When we finally arrived home, we were tired.

Something had happened to me during Communion. I ate of the bread . . . and was filled. I did not wish to share the experience until I could rummage around in the blanket chest and find my Bible and look up the Emmaus story. If I remembered correctly, after Jesus blessed and broke the bread and shared it with the disciples, their eyes were opened.

From that moment on, I began to understand not *what* had been missing from my life, but *who*. The transcendent Christ! The living, breathing Son of God who surrendered His life on the cross to redeem mankind.

The Christ outside of us who speaks through Scripture and prayer.

Half a year passed, and then one day Lindsay drew me aside and said, "I want to be reinstated in the active ministry. That verse from Hebrews keeps running through my head: 'Thou art a priest forever after the order of Melchizedek.'[20] I don't know what it will take, or how long it will be before I'm allowed to serve at the altar again."

"We'll be moving ahead into something new," I assured him. "It's like our marriage. We couldn't go back to the old marriage. Things keep changing." Then I added tearily, "I saved your preaching stoles. I couldn't bear to give them away."

There would be an appointment with the new bishop—two years of appointments, in fact. "You've been away for a long time," he reminded Lindsay. "Make sure this is a firm decision. Serve in a lay capacity first for a year. After that, if you are certain you want to be reinstated to the priesthood, we'll start working out the procedure."

The garden had taught me about waiting. Nevertheless, it was difficult to be patient, once our minds were made up. In the end we were glad the bishop moved cautiously, insisting on a time of testing.

We were grateful for the love our Quaker friends had given to us, and the spiritual sustenance. At first, after breaking our news, we promised to come back frequently. It did not turn out to be feasible to attempt worship alternately in two places. We needed to become part of a congregation again if Lindsay's decision was to be taken seriously by those in authority, and so we chose to attend the services at Grace Memorial Church, a few blocks from our home.

In returning to orthodox Christianity, I found, at last, that for which I hungered: Jesus Christ. I was so starved for the Word of God that sometimes I read an entire book of the Bible through from beginning to end without stopping. The stories and parables I'd known in childhood, the sayings of Jesus, the miracles, the Psalms, every Bible verse was fresh and new like the flowers springing up in my garden.

After several years of gardening, I had not tired of seeing hyacinth, daffodil, rose and dahlia bloom another time. Never once had I wearied of the crisp, sweet taste of corn on the cob or homegrown tomatoes. That is how I felt about verses of Scripture. The Bible had become my spiritual garden.

The cross, which once had seemed so irrelevant, so absurd, made sense out of life now. Love broken, rejected, redeemed. The Quakers taught that the crucifixion happened once, two thousand years ago; but now I grew to understand that it happened daily, followed by the resurrection experience. I learned that when we return, with forgiveness and love, to the community or person who hurt us most, we come face-to-face with the risen Christ.

After months of waiting and work and prayer, my husband was reinstated in active ministry. Over 250 friends and clergy brethren attended the moving evening service. It was late May, warm and clear, and dusk had just started to fall. Glancing around the large old church, I saw there was standing room only, and my eyes filled as I recognized neighbors and their children, Quakers, Baptists, Roman Catholics, Presbyterians and Jews. Slowly and solemnly, the procession started down the aisle as voices thundered the uplifting words of the ancient hymn, "Come Holy Ghost, Creator Blest." The choir seemed to be enormous that night, and in the front pews sat another "choir" of clergy who were not officiating in the service.

Before the bishop examined Lindsay and prayed the prayers of restoration, a good friend, the Rev. Renne Harris, preached a brief but powerful sermon, ending with the following words:

"When we lose our concept of God, we cannot lose God. It means that when we encounter diabolus, he who would shatter and break us apart, that Jesus, the Bread of Life, will be with us to nurture and sustain and restore us. And when it seems that all is lost and there is no way out and the wait is interminable, we are fed by Jesus; and like Elijah, in the strength of that food we can go on, even forty days and forty nights, to Horeb, the Mountain of God.

"Such is the faith we this night celebrate!"

For me, that night, the Communion truly was the Bread of Life!

A little later, we crowded into the parish hall to hug and kiss, to receive the delighted congratulations of friends. I pushed my way through the mob to find first Lindsay, and then the bishop, and Jay, the pastor of Grace Memorial Church who had affirmed our faith during the long two-year wait.

We thought we could never be happier. But wait, there is more! Two weeks after that landmark occasion, Lindsay attended a special healing conference. I joined him there on the college campus for the evening service.

I could hear music ringing out from the chapel long before I saw the building itself. I stood on the porch for a moment in the evening light before entering. Hundreds of faces were lit with joy. Arms raised, many of the people abandoned themselves unashamedly to praise. This was my first experience of the renewal wrought by the Holy Spirit during my absence from the faith: a renewal unconfined. Here before me, worshiping together, were brothers and sisters of the universal Church.

That evening I met the third person of the Trinity, the Holy Spirit. In some ways He seemed strangely familiar, for it was He who had led me, lo these many years. But tonight I became acquainted with the way He could unite the faithful with the power of healing love.

In that moment I knew, without a doubt, that I was standing where I wanted to be. I had come home.

Endnotes

1 Dante Alighieri, *The Divine Comedy* (Inferno), trans. by John Ciardi, New American Library (Mentor Books), *Times Mirror*, 1954, p. 28.

2 Jung, C. G. *Psyche and Symbol* (Commentary on *The Secret of the Golden Flower*, ed. by Laszlo, Doubleday Anchor Books, Garden City, N.Y., 1958, p. 313.

3 Carroll, Lewis, *Alice in Wonderland*, Liveright, Inc., N.Y., 1932, p. 65.

4 Carroll, Lewis, *Through the Looking Glass*, Liveright, Inc., N.Y., 1932, p. 230.

5 Eliot, T. S., *Four Quartets*, "Little Gidding," Harcourt, Brace, N.Y., 1942, p. 34.

6 Matthew 7:7, RSV.

7 Psalm 18:2, RSV.

8 Deuteronomy 32:18, RSV.

9 Chardin, Teilhard, *Science and Christ*, Harper & Row, N.Y., 1965, p. 12.

10 Genesis 1:2, RSV.

11 Blake, William, *The Poetry and Prose of William Blake*, "Four Zoas," ed. by David Erdman, Doubleday, Garden City, N.Y., 1965, p. 318.

[12] Thoreau, Henry D., *Walden*, Houghton Mifflin, Boston, 1854, p. 506.

[13] Thoreau, Henry D., "Autumn" (from the journals of Thoreau, ed. by H. G. O. Blake, Houghton Mifflin, Boston, 1892, entry for Nov. 3, 1853.

[14] The Bhagavad-Gita, trans. by Swami Prabhavananda and Christopher Isherwood, New American Library (Mentor Books), 1956, p. 45.

[15] Kelly, Thomas, *Testament of Devotion*, Harper & Row, N.Y., 1943, p. 116.

[16] Dante Alighieri, *The Divine Comedy* (Paradise), trans. by Dorothy Sayers and Barbara Reynolds, Penguin Books, Baltimore, 1962, Canto 30, p. 319.

[17] John 8:12, RSV.

[18] John 1:5, RSV.

[19] Revelation 21:23, RSV.

[20] Hebrews 5:6, RSV.

CHRISTIAN HERALD ASSOCIATION AND ITS MINISTRIES

CHRISTIAN HERALD ASSOCIATION, founded in 1878, publishes The Christian Herald Magazine, one of the leading interdenominational religious monthlies in America. Through its wide circulation, it brings inspiring articles and the latest news of religious developments to many families. From the magazine's pages came the initiative for CHRISTIAN HERALD CHILDREN'S HOME and THE BOWERY MISSION, two individually supported not-for-profit corporations.

CHRISTIAN HERALD CHILDREN'S HOME, established in 1894, is the name for a unique and dynamic ministry to disadvantaged children, offering hope and opportunities which would not otherwise be available for reasons of poverty and neglect. The goal is to develop each child's potential and to demonstrate Christian compassion and understanding to children in need.

Mont Lawn is a permanent camp located in Bushkill, Pennsylvania. It is the focal point of a ministry which provides a healthful "vacation with a purpose" to children who without it would be confined to the streets of the city. Up to 1000 children between the ages of 7 and 11 come to Mont Lawn each year.

Christian Herald Children's Home maintains year-round contact with children by means of an *In-City Youth Ministry*. Central to its philosophy is the belief that only through sustained relationships and demonstrated concern can individual lives be truly enriched. Special emphasis is on individual guidance, spiritual and family counseling and tutoring. This follow-up ministry to inner-city children culminates for many in financial assistance toward higher education and career counseling.

THE BOWERY MISSION, located at 227 Bowery, New York City, has since 1879 been reaching out to the lost men on the Bowery, offering them what could be their last chance to rebuild their lives. Every man is fed, clothed and ministered to. Countless numbers have entered the 90-day residential rehabilitation program at the Bowery Mission. A concentrated ministry of counseling, medical care, nutrition therapy, Bible study and Gospel services awakens a man to spiritual renewal within himself.

These ministries are supported solely by the voluntary contributions of individuals and by legacies and bequests. Contributions are tax deductible. Checks should be made out either to CHRISTIAN HERALD CHILDREN'S HOME or to THE BOWERY MISSION.

Administrative Office: 40 Overlook Drive, Chappaqua, New York 10514
Telephone: (914) 769-9000